RISK/BENEFIT ANALYSIS

RISK / BENEFIT ANALYSIS

EDMUND A.C. CROUCH
RICHARD WILSON

BALLINGER PUBLISHING COMPANY
Cambridge, Massachusetts
A Subsidiary of Harper & Row, Publishers, Inc.

International Standard Book Number: 0-88410-667-5

Library of Congress Catalog Card Number: 81-22832

Printed in the United States of America

Library of Congress Cataloging in Publication Data

Crouch, Edmund A. C.
  Risk/benefit analysis.

  Bibliography: p.
  Includes index.
  1. Risk-Evaluation. 2. Risk management. I. Wilson,
Richard, 1926–   II. Title.
HD61.C77   658.4'03   81-22832
ISBN 0-88410-667-5   AACR2

CONTENTS

v

LIST OF FIGURES

LIST OF TABLES

PREFACE

One role of government is to enable citizens to undertake tasks jointly that they cannot undertake separately; another is to protect individual citizens from the actions of others. There is a dilemma here, recognized as early as Tacitus, who in the fifteenth volume of his Annals noted that "The desire for safety lies over and against every great and noble enterprise." Sometimes the tasks that are undertaken jointly can adversely affect the individual. It is the task of risk analysis to resolve this dilemma. America is in many respects the safest country in the world. It did not get that way by accident, for there is great attention paid to safety in every aspect of society. We hope that this book will assist in the continued effort required to make life safer.

Although the book is entitled *Risk/Benefit Analysis*, the major emphasis is on the more restricted field called risk assessment. The word "analysis" is used to describe the whole process of considering risks, including the making of decisions. A risk assessor is a person who organizes data in such a way that others can make decisions more reliably. The assessor should not, in his assessment, try to influence the decision, although that is often done. The following example shows one reason for such bias.

Two scientists A and B might argue about what level of risk to human health is posed by air pollution at 1980 levels. Scientist A might say zero; scientist B might say 1 in 10,000 per year. Both would probably agree that reducing air pollution is worth an expenditure of $100 million per year, and would be willing to say just that. To that extent this is inconsistent with scientist A's statement of zero risk; A fears that if he or she gives any finite number, then too much money would be spent, and thus gives a biased number (zero). With a careful definition of the risk assessment task, separate from the task of making a decision, this problem can be avoided.

It is now clear that many segments of society wish to have some influence in decisions on matters involving risks. With a separate risk assessor and decisionmaker, the risk assessor is free to be as objective as possible, while the decisionmaker is free to be swayed by the value judgments of these many segments, as is right and proper.

A distinguished medical statistician recently asked one of us why we waste our time with risk analysis. "All you are doing is replacing total garbage by partial garbage." Even in this critical comment there is a positive note, but we hope that the pages that follow do not contain even partial garbage. To that end we have attempted to highlight the assumptions and difficulties of interpretation, and to provide a road map through an intricate area.

We are unashamed proponents of calculating numbers wherever possible. Without such calculations, we cannot be sure that the risk assessor has thought through the problem at all. Of course, a number can be stripped of the uncertainty estimates and misused, but a noun or verb in any piece of descriptive prose can also be stripped of its qualifying adjectives or adverbs. Despite our emphasis on numeracy in risk assessment, it is necessary to warn against the tendency to overburden decisionmakers with intricate details of the arithmetic processes used in arriving at the numerical results. What is required by a decisionmaker is a concise statement of numerical results, their uncertainties, and the simplifying assumptions made in deriving such results. But most important of all is a statement of the areas in which no numerical results are possible so that value judgments are required.

ACKNOWLEDGMENTS

This book developed from work done for the Energy Research and Development Agency (now the Department of Energy) via a subcontract through the Brookhaven National Laboratory. Subsequent partial financial help was received from many sources, including the General Electric Foundation, the Cabot Corporation, Monsanto, and Dow Chemical. Their support is gratefully acknowledged. In the initial stages Dr. Andrew Van Horn was a principal author, and we are grateful for the help and inspiration he supplied. We had many fruitful discussions on risk with colleagues, among whom we would particularly like to thank Drs. L. Hamilton, H. Raiffa, M. Weinstein, J. Menkart, D. Okrent, and P. Slovic.

1 PERSPECTIVE ON RISK

We are not prepared to go to limitless expense to save lives that could be saved on the basis of the technical knowledge we possess.

Editorial, *The Observer* (London),
14 January, 1968,

Life is a risky business. We are all continuously facing risks of some sort or another. Sometimes we face risky monetary decisions; sometimes dangers to life and limb. Not only do we face these dangers, we daily make decisions about them after comparing the risk to the benefit. Each morning one decides to get up, face the world and the boss, forgoing the benefit of a day in bed but avoiding the risk of being fired and the cost of lost salary. One decides when it is safe to cross the road and when it is wiser to wait; one may choose to ride by automobile rather than bicycle or walk, to wear safety glasses while home woodworking, or to quit smoking.

In these and all the other everyday choices consciously or unconsciously made, one assesses the risk more or less crudely, assesses the benefits of monetary gain, pleasure, or other objectives, and makes one's own trade-off. This instant risk/cost/benefit analysis is based on a host of factors including reasoning, guess work, and past experience. In many obvious cases, the actual risks are small, so that the risk assessment need be done only crudely and perfunctorily to be adequate, but even the crudest analysis can affect decisions. Two

1

individuals may reach different decisions on the timing for crossing the street, because different individuals may not agree on the values they apply to different risks. Moreover, these values may not remain constant in even one person.

This book introduces some of the ideas and difficulties associated with attempts to perform formal risk assessments and make risk/benefit comparisons. The risks discussed are to individual and group human welfare. It is plausible for other species to be of interest, but usually the survival and welfare of the whole population of another species, not individuals or particular groups, are of concern. Although risks to other species may be included in a risk/cost/benefit analysis, in the monetary or nonmonetary analysis of benefits and costs, the concern is usually for the ultimate indirect effects on human beings of direct effects on the other species.

The word *risk* implies uncertainty, so risk analysts do not discuss situations with certain outcomes, although uncertainties can arise in many different ways. One's uncertainty about involvement in automobile accidents does not arise because one does not know whether cars are involved in accidents, but because one does not know whether one's own car will be involved in an accident. In other cases the risks are hypothetical—it is not known whether the event actually occurs; much uncertainty arises this way. Saccharin at high doses causes bladder cancer in rats, but there is no strong direct evidence that it causes cancer in human beings at low doses, although it is prudent to make the hypothetical assumption that it does. Individuals consuming saccharin are faced with an uncertainty of a different kind from that in the automobile example. We shall in most of this book ignore such differences, however, because all such uncertainties may be formally treated in the same way.

Any events or actions that pose a possible risk to human beings are perceived through the filter of the senses. Further, perceptions are modified by experience, time of occurrence, culture, religion, and other variables that make each individual unique. Evidently the assignment of the same values to similar risks by different persons cannot be expected a priori. The experience of attempting to cross a street in an unfamiliar city is an example: An inhabitant clearly recognizes a "safe" situation, where the visitor hesitates. The results represent a difference of opinion, each individual basing logical opinion on perceptions of risk, but differing from all others with different perceptions. For a discussion of risk perception see Chapter 4.

The importance of perceptions of risks is illustrated by Table 1–1, which summarizes results of a public opinion survey. Most people seem to believe that life is becoming more dangerous, even though most objective measures show the contrary to be true. The expectation of life, for example, an inverse measure of the probability of dying, has steadily increased, from perhaps twenty-eight years fifteen centuries ago, to fifty years one century ago, to about seventy-two years currently, although the rate of increase has been decreasing. The increase has been brought about by the elimination of many large risks to life, among them many infectious and contagious diseases, poor working conditions, and inadequate nutrition. Figure 1–1 shows the reduction in death rates in this century by age group. Detailed examination shows that the increase since 1960 in the 15 to 24 age group is due to automobile accidents. Doll (1979) has also shown how health, as measured by most medical indicators, is improving. It is now necessary to concentrate on the many smaller risks, often poorly understood, in order to further reduce total risks. Perhaps it is

Table 1–1. Public Opinion Survey Comparing Risk Today to Risk of Twenty Years Ago.

Q: Thinking about the *actual amount of risk* facing our society, would you say that people are subject to more risk today than they were twenty years ago, less risk today, or about the same amount of risk today as twenty years ago?

Q: I'd like to start by asking you a few questions about the amount of risk we face in our day-to-day living. Thinking about the *actual amount of risk* facing our society, would you say people are subject to more risk today than they were twenty years ago, less risk today, or about the same amount of risk today as twenty years ago?

	Top Corporate Executives (N = 401)	Investors, Lenders (N = 104)	Congress (N = 47)	Federal Regulators (N = 47)	Public (N = 1,488)
	(percent)				
More risk	38	60	55	43	78
Less risk	36	13	26	13	6
Same amount	24	26	19	40	14
Not sure	1	1	. . .	4	2

Source: Marsh & McLennan Companies (1980).

Figure 1-1.   Death Rates at Five Year Intervals from 1900 to 1975 for Various Age Groups: United States.

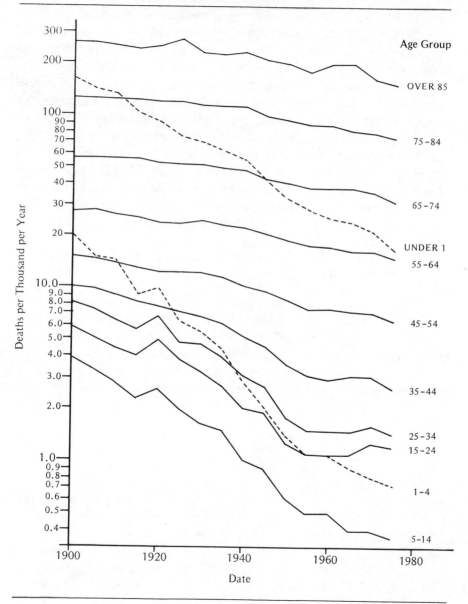

the necessity of discussing many more risks, even though smaller, that has caused the apparent alarm of the respondents in Table 1-1, who are counting incidents by number only and failing to note their magnitudes.

It is the differing perceptions and opinions of individuals and groups that control their actions. When a single action has a small possible consequence—a maximum of one death at a time—and the action is repeated by large numbers of individuals, these differences lead to results from good to bad, but no single action can have a catastrophic effect. Individuals can see not only the results of their own actions, but also the results of the ill-conceived actions of others. They can then adjust their future behavior to reduce the harmful effects. Modern technological systems are so large that a single decision might result in large harmful effects—several thousands of deaths; with little or no opportunity for this feedback to limit harmful effects, the first wrong action might be disastrous, when compared with historical precedents. Hence it is desirable to find out how risky an action is before anyone has performed it and to attain some objectivity in the analysis of risk, instead of relying on imperfect and uninformed direct perception. Objectivity is introduced in an attempt to modify a priori perceptions by the use of objective evidence. It is necessary always to bear in mind that any such analytical attempt attacks only one aspect of any problem: The risks of any event or action have always to be weighed against costs and benefits.

We regard this introduction of objectivity as essential for a sound decision. Unless the analyst has calculated a risk, with its uncertainty, outlined the analytic procedure, and emphasized the omissions, others cannot be sure he or she has thought about the problem at all. Chapter 3 therefore, goes into some detail on different ways of calculating (assessing) risks.

Having objectively evaluated risks of events or actions, what should the analyst do with the results? It is usually desirable to compare risks of one set of events or actions with those of a different set designed to achieve the same or similar ends. It may be straightforward to compare risks, but usually the risks are only one measure of effectiveness of an action, so that the harder job of trying to compare risks with costs and benefits must be essayed. Chapter 5 introduces the concepts required for tackling this task somewhat formally, but when the formalism is dissected it reduces to common sense plus arithmetic. Knowing how and where to use the arithmetic is straightforward—it is the common sense that must continuously be referred to.

Chapter 6 outlines nine cases where some person(s) or agency— official or private—has attempted to use a risk analysis in decision-making. These published analyses are all incomplete in our view, and we enumerate some of the omissions that we see. Myriad decisions are made without formal written or published justification. We suspect that such decisions are even more likely to be flawed in their treatment of risk. A decision process open to public discussion and review has a lot to commend it, the decision on the use of saccharin being a particular example that has markedly increased public understanding of risk.

There is a considerable degree of agreement that a comparison of risks and benefits is necessary. For example, Russell Train, administrator of the U.S. Environmental Protection Agency, said:

> Once the detailed risk and benefit analyses are available, I must consider the extent of the risk, the benefits conferred by the substance, the availability of substitutes and the costs of control of the substance. On the basis of careful review, I may determine that the risks are so small or the benefits so great that no action or only limited action is warranted. Conversely, I may decide that the risks of some or all uses exceed the benefits and that stronger action is essential (Train 1976: 41FR41102).

An official U.K. Report agrees:

> An important area for further research is the quantitative assessment of accident probability. . . . The approach can be applied at various levels to a wide variety of problems as a contribution towards establishing priorities on an objective and systematic basis (Report of the Committee on Health and Safety at Work 1972: paragraph 44).

John Higginson, Director of the International Agency for Research on Cancer has stated:

> In accepting [risk] we should be guided by common sense and honesty. We should not subject others knowingly to risks that we would not accept for ourselves or for our families. The decisions on socially acceptable risks which imply the calculation of costs/benefits should not necessarily be confined to an elite group but rather be established through a consensus of society as a whole and/or its representatives assisted by experts (Higginson 1976: 361).

The important role of balance in the political decision is stressed by those actually responsible for environmental protection. Thus

K. Mellanby, Director of the Monks Wood Experimental Station of the English Nature Conservancy and Editor of the Journal of Environmental Pollution, writes:

> Some ecologists harm their cause by overstating their case and by condemning any industrial development even if they do not hesitate to make use of the products of that industry! We need to recognize 'real' risks, and to concentrate on eliminating them while at the same time using our technology properly for the benefit of mankind (Mellanby 1971).

One of the advantages of a logical procedure of risk analysis is that it can reduce polarization. John Dunster, Deputy Director General of the (U.K.) Health and Safety Executive, says:

> Some risks are clearly so unacceptable that they must be eliminated. Others, less severe or less likely should be reduced to the point where the benefits of the risky activity balance the costs of its ill effects. Striking the balance invariably involves compromise (Dunster 1977: 454).

Most people recognize that decisionmaking is not performed by the experts in risk assessment: "Balancing the benefits against the risks belongs not in the domain of science but to society. The judgment is a value judgment—a social rather than a scientific decision." (Commoner 1977: 73).

Chapter 7 presents a catalogue of risks that we have assembled. Each is instructive in some way; some (like cigarette smoking) can obviously be reduced that are not being reduced; others are small yet cause public alarm. We hope that by presenting them together here some degree of perspective can be obtained.

Chapter 8 discusses some problems of managing or mitigating risks—risks must be managed because they cannot be entirely eliminated.

The last section of the book is a bibliography of books and articles on risk and benefit, some of which may be of interest for further reading.

REFERENCES

Commoner, B. 1977. *New York Times Magazine* (September 25): 73.

Doll, R. 1979. "The Pattern of Disease in the Post Infection Era, National Trends." Proceedings of the Royal Society of London B205: 47.

Dunster, J. 1977. "The Risk Equations: Virtue in Compromise." *New Scientist* 74 (May): 454.

Higginson, J. 1976. "A Hazardous Society? Individual Versus Community Responsibility in Cancer Protection." Third Annual B. Rosenhaus Lecture, *American Journal of Public Health* 66: 361.

Marsh McLennan Companies. 1980. "Risks in a Complex Society." Public Opinion Poll carried out by Lewis Harris and Associates, New York.

Mellanby, K. 1971. "Unwise Use of Chemicals." Keynote paper in 1st International Conference on the Environmental Future, Finland, edited by N. Polunin. New York: Barnes and Noble, Inc.

Report of the Committee on Health and Safety at Work (Chairman Lord Robens). 1972. Paragraph 44. London: Her Majesty's Stationery Office.

Train, R. 1976. In the Federal Register, 41FR41102, Tuesday, May 25.

U.S. Bureau of the Census. 1975. *Historical Statistics of the United States, Colonial Times to 1970.* Washington, D.C.

2 THE MEANING OF RISK

Risk is a word used in many different ways by different disciplines. Indeed so varied is its use that some authors have avoided the word entirely. We consider it necessary to define precisely what we mean by a risk and by its numerical measurement.

Although there are uses of the word *risk* that are more inclusive, in this book we associate risks with events or actions. (Note that inaction, whether it is conscious or unconscious, is also susceptible to analysis—for example, the effects of a decision to take no action on CO_2 buildup in the atmosphere might be analyzed). The events and actions may be small or large, from digging one shovel of dirt to creating new seas, from creating a one-way street to decisions on whole highway construction programs. For each event or action we associate some units of risk, leading to a risk per street crossing, for example, or a risk per ton of copper ore mined. Thus in some way we have a visualization as follows:

Total risk = (How much or how often) $\otimes$ (Some risk per unit of action, or per event) .

In a more useful form, we can write:

Risk = Probability $\otimes$ Severity.

For decision making, the amount or severity of risk perceived is used as an approximation of the risk itself; so the terms of the foregoing equation represent perceptions, and the equation reads: "Our perception of the magnitude of risk from some event depends on some form of product of how often we think the event will occur and how serious we consider each occurrence to be in its effects."

To illustrate, consider the following cases:

1. The risk of a broken leg is greater for an inexperienced skier than for an experienced skier.
2. The risk of death or injury in automobile accidents is greater for those not wearing restraint harnesses (seat belts) than for those who are.

In (1), the severity of injury (a broken leg) is the same, but we expect the probability to be higher for the inexperienced skier. In (2), we expect the probability of accidents is approximately the same, but the severity to be markedly higher for the unrestrained automobile occupants.

Notice that we have carefully refrained from putting an ordinary multiplication sign ($\times$) in the equation, for in some practical cases risk perceptions may not be truly multiplicative. Most risks do have some multiplicative features, though, which we shall use in our first attempt to introduce objectivity.

Thus far, the discussion has been concerned mainly with single events or actions. Since the definition has been left open, such single events or actions could cover most cases, but in essence they consist of the most elementary actions to be analyzed with respect to their risk content. To associate a risk with more complex events or actions, it is necessary to break down the actions into individual smaller actions, the summation of which is usually assumed to be possible.

$$\text{Risk} = S\,(\text{Probability} \otimes \text{Severity} \otimes \text{Weight})\ ,$$

where the S stands for whatever form of addition (unknown) is actually used by individuals. The weight factor is included separately here; it could perhaps be included in the severity term if the equation relates perceptions, but it is convenient for later discussion to isolate it. It is included to account for the possibility that in evaluating a problem consisting of many different parts, risks of apparently similar magnitude may be accorded very different weights in consideration of the totality.

Any inappropriate assignment of weight or erroneous perception of the risk of any section of a problem may lead to inappropriate ("wrong") actions or decisions. Such actions or decisions would result in end results different from those planned and thus not optimum from some point of view. One attempt at reducing such possibilities is the objective analysis of risk, which is pursued throughout this book.

To make any start on objective assessment it is necessary to realize what is being measured. Death is one clear objective measure. The total annual risk of death at any age is just the probability of dying within one year. In the absence of any extra causes, population averages for this measure are obtained from national mortality tables (see Chapter 7). But in risk assessments we are interested in additional risks of death or components of the total risk of death due to some specific actions undertaken either voluntarily or involuntarily. More often, we are interested in how much of an action to undertake, so that we wish to evaluate measures such as extra probability of death per unit of action (per cigarette smoked, or per ton of coal mined, for example).

Death is not the only measure of risk of interest, for, although it is probably the most objective one and for this reason often used, it may not capture large components of what are perceived as risks. In balanced decisions it may become vital to consider other measures. A few possible such measures are:

Deaths
{ by age
  by cause
  ⋮

Injuries
{ by cause
  by type
  by severity index
  ⋮

Illness
{ by cause
  by type
  by severity index
  ⋮

Man-days lost
{ by cause
  ⋮

Days of impaired health
Days of pain
Loss of life expectancy

Total numbers (whole task) or probabilities (for individuals)

per unit operation size

per event

per unit dose
  (per cigarette,
   per ton produced,
   per unit output,
   etc.)

Figure 2-1. Accidental Deaths per Million Tons of Coal Mined in the United States.

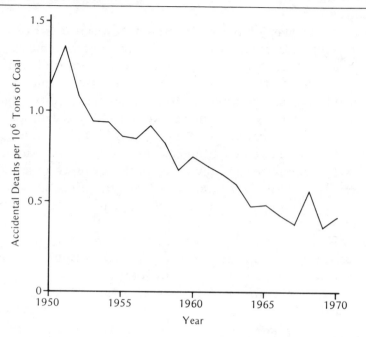

What measures of risk are appropriate for a particular risk assessment depend on the specific details of the question the assessment is designed to illuminate. Presumably they will be the measures corresponding as nearly as possible to the way in which the risks are perceived. In what follows we will usually be limiting consideration to risks of death (measured by probabilities of dying or expected excess numbers of deaths) resulting from various actions, although other risks will occasionally be mentioned.

Although we shall not concern ourselves much with it, the distinction between risks and measures of risk is not totally academic. A simple example is the American coal industry, taken as a whole, between 1950 and 1970. Figure 2-1 is a plot of one measure of risk in this industry—the number of accidental deaths per million tons of coal mined. Clearly this measure steadily declined during this period, so that, if we follow the industry through successive years, it appears to be getting safer. Looking at Figure 2-2, which shows the behavior of another measure of risk—the number of accidental deaths per

Figure 2-2. Accidental Deaths per Thousand Coal Mine Employees in the United States.

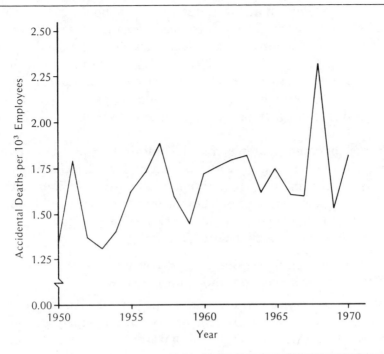

thousand persons employed—one might naively assert that the industry is getting more dangerous, not safer.

Evidently the two measures illustrated might be used to support opposing views on the safety of coal mining. Neither measure taken alone is right or wrong, nor are they even contradictory even though they may be so perceived. Any risk assessment supposed to be complete would have to draw attention to the two aspects of the risk of coal mining gauged by the two different measures and would have to take both into account, depending exactly on the purpose of the risk assessment. From a national point of view, given that a certain amount of coal has to be obtained, deaths per million tons of coal is the more appropriate measure of risk, whereas from a labor leader's point of view, deaths per thousand persons employed may be more relevant.

What steps to take to reduce the risk will depend on which of the two measures is used. Doubling the number of miners, each working on alternate days, for example, would decrease the risk per miner by a factor of 2, but the risk per ton of coal mined would stay constant. In decision making both measures and both points of view would usually have to be considered. Although a regulator is primarily interested in the total impact on society (risk per ton mined), it is not consistent with a stable society for one group to face a much larger total risk than another group. In comparing risk and benefits we naturally consider both groups; those engaged in particularly hazardous occupations get higher pay to compensate the increased risk by an increased benefit.

In the foregoing example of accidental death, the risks due to coal mining have been vastly oversimplified and we have ignored other aspects of the industry that should be considered simultaneously. Coal mining was treated as one homogeneous industry, and only accidental deaths of employees were included in the measures of risk used. We have completely ignored, inter alia:

- Risk to the public—from dust and water emissions, from subsidence, and from coal transport, for example.

- Variations between groups within the industry. Underground and surface workers face different hazards in the underground part of the industry, and similarly the hazards to those in strip mining (surface) operations differ.

- Other measures of risk. There are other risks of death from, for example, pneumoconiosis (black lung disease) and other components of risk ranging from the risks of traveling to work, through injuries and illnesses.

Evidently, death is only a partial measure of risk, and for the best understanding of risk as many partial measures as possible should be evaluated. Although it would be possible to aggregate all such measures arithmetically in some way, they would have to be added together with some weighting factors relating different measures, as by using the formulas stated earlier, but with arithmetic summation and multiplication. Weighting of different measures is necessarily somewhat arbitrary and furthermore may usurp clear perceptual differences. The arbitrariness is easy to illustrate by attempting to find a weighting factor to relate deaths and man-days lost (MDL).

Accidents occur at all ages, but the average age of persons dying of accidents is forty-two compared with an average age of death of seventy-two for society as a whole in the United States. The loss of working life expectancy is thus about twenty-five years (taking account of retirement), leading to 25 × 300 = 7,500 man-days lost per death. But the average age for cancer deaths is about fifty-four, so the loss of working life expectancy is thirteen years or 3,900 MDL per death. Any weighting factor would thus strictly have to depend on the cause of death, although an average of 6,000 MDL per death is often used—and whether such an average is adequate will depend on the particular case. These estimates do not assist in our problem particularly, for we do not necessarily perceive death as being simply equivalent to a loss of a certain number of working days! The measure takes no account of nonworking time, for one thing. Moreover, depending on the question being answered by the risk assessment, the average may not be of interest—it may be that individual variations are of more importance.

With these caveats on measures of risk we return to objective risk assessment. The measures chosen must be evaluated for the action or event under study. The straightforward way of doing this is to break down each action or event into components until each part may be taken as a whole, to evaluate the risk measure for each, and then to sum to obtain the resultant measure of risk for the original action or event. Obviously the depth of analysis can vary, depending on the problem and on the analyst, but the first essential is identification of parts that can be treated individually. The example of coal mining accidents has been treated as a component and averaged over all employees, although of course it would be possible to dissect it further and separately analyze risks to miners underground, surface workers, office workers, and others, and to include other risks.

It would appear that, having broken the action or event into components, analyzed each component, and summed again, one has obtained the measure of risk for the complete action or event. This statement is not quite true, however, or, rather, it is incomplete. Consider a single action, with the possibility of its being either carried out or not. In the first case, the procedure evaluates some measure(s) of risk for performing the action. Even if the action is not carried out, it is likely that there will still be some risks to the persons who would be affected by the action. There is thus an arbitrary choice in a risk assessment: Should such a "background level" of risk be subtracted from each evaluated measure to account for the risks that would be present even in the absence of the action or event being assessed?

The problem posed refers to the case of a simple decision: to do or to refrain. If the decision is between two or more alternatives, a similar problem arises as soon as any attempt is made to make any comparison: Should the comparison be based on absolute or on incremental measures of risk? The importance of this question becomes obvious when it is realized that comparisons based on the first may give different results from those based on the second. An example shows this:

Consider two alternative actions A and B, either of which involves changing the status of some of the N people in the population. Prior to any action the populace is subject to some background risk with a measure ξ per person. If action A involves increasing the risk to $N/2$ people to 1.1ξ, whereas action B increases the risk to $N/3$ people to 1.2ξ, the results differ depending on whether absolute risk or incremental risk is analyzed.

First look at the absolute risks of actions A and B.

For A the absolute risk is $N/2 \times 1.1\xi = 0.55N\xi$.

For B it is $N/3 \times 1.2\xi = 0.4N\xi$ ',

whence risk of $A >$ risk of B. But now look at incremental risks.

For A $N/2 \times (1.1 - 1)\xi = 0.05N\xi$

For B $N/3 \times (1.2 - 1)\xi = 0.066N\xi$

whence, risk of $B >$ risk of A, a result apparently at variance with the one previously obtained.

The preceding example was constructed to be clear cut and obvious. In practice, one could not treat the whole population as homogeneous and facing similar risks; similarly, the workforces on the projects would not be homogeneous. Thus computation of the risks would require some form of averaging over different occupations. It would also be difficult and ambiguous actually to compute the value of any incremental measure of risk, for in general in considering any given project, the problem of what the rest of the economy is doing is ignored, so that an indirect approach to the incremental risk computation is required by hypothetically redistributing into the economy the resources used in the project. How such redistribution should be performed introduces the ambiguity.

Using the preceding example as the model, one would redistribute the manpower throughout the economy, presumably in proportion to the manpower present already in the economy minus the project, and compute the risk measure to the redistributed manpower (and any concomitant risks to others) as the background level. It can be argued, however, that the relevant redistribution method should be to assign the capital cost of the project to various sectors of the economy, and compute the value of the risk measure associated with this capital in the rest of the economy as the background level. One can similarly argue for redistribution on the basis of almost any characteristic of the project (two further examples being materials use and manhours).

Such different methods of computation of background risk lead to different estimates of it, and even if a common method is used, two different projects will have different levels of background risk. The ambiguity and difficulty of computation thus make it essential that, in cases where incremental risk measures are desired, the projects be defined clearly and the method of computation made abundantly clear, with results from alternative methods preferably presented simultaneously to indicate the sensitivity to such alternatives.

Although the foregoing discussion has demonstrated the problems inherent in definition and computation of incremental measures of risk, it has not answered the question of whether such measures are appropriate. Once again, the appropriateness of the measure depends on the precise question to which an answer is desired. For assessing risks to a whole society, presumably with the object of minimizing them, an incremental measure is clearly more appropriate than a total measure for any given action, since the alternatives to any given action, even inaction, must always be considered, so that the problem becomes one of differential riskiness. In other cases, however, total risks are far more relevant. An individual company concerned with its safety record may be interested in the total risks of its actions, as may individual persons or labor leaders.

The problem just considered is but one, albeit an important one, that may arise from lack of definition of system boundaries. In the evaluation of a measure of risk for any action, event, or project—that is, for any system—the value obtained depends on the boundaries set to that system, on which parts are included and which excluded. In evaluating total risks in the foregoing problem, we were effectively trying to draw a boundary around some set of actions or events or geographical regions and to evaluate the mesures of risk of interest within that boundary. To evaluate a differential risk, in the ideal case a boundary is drawn around all actions or events and the relevant measure(s) of risk are evaluated for everything in two cases, the first with the project, the second without, and then the second is subtracted from the first to obtain a differential measure.

Let us look a little more closely at the earlier example, the coal industry. Figures 2-1 and 2-2 graphed two measures of risk for the coal industry, accidental deaths per million tons mined and accidental deaths per thousand persons employed, for twenty years. Although it was not explicitly stated, we assumed a certain system boundary in presenting those risk measures. The system boundary enclosed the U.S. coal industry (defined by a Standard Industrial Classification number), including office workers and coal face workers together, including open cast and underground mines together, and including bituminous coal and anthracite together but was limited to deaths among those working in this industry only. To be more complete, it would also be necessary to include accidental deaths in other industries due to the requirements of the coal industry. (Note that we are still limiting ourselves to the single measure, accidental deaths.) The coal industry uses machinery, which in turn uses iron and steel; and accidental deaths occur in the machinery production industry, in the iron and steel industry, in iron ore mining, and in transport between these. Some of these accidental deaths may thus be ascribed to coal production. Similarly the coal industry uses some electricity bought from the electrical utility industry, in which there occur accidental deaths also, some of which may also be ascribed to the coal industry.

A complication is that both the iron and steel industry and the electricity industry use coal, so it would appear that carrying the argument an extra step leads to circularity. But the analysis is not circular, because not all the coal is used in iron and steel and electricity production. One way of describing the situation is to say that the series obtained is convergent. The same problem is met in the discipline of net energy analysis and is similarly solved (mathematically) by solving coupled sets of equations. The result is a change in the evaluated magnitude of the measure of risk, but this is to be expected since the system under analysis (defined by the system boundaries) has now been enlarged to include those portions of the electricity supply industry and the iron and steel industry required to keep the coal industry in operation.

As in net energy analysis, there may be some ambiguity in risk analyses on systems such as that just described. It is usual to assume that all parts of the system are linear (an increase of output of any industry of x percent requires increases of all its inputs by x percent) unless better models are available. If some operation has multiple outputs, it is difficult or impossible to assign risks unambiguously to each output. But with suitable choice of system boundary, such ambiguities can perhaps be minimized in their impact on the total measures of risks being sought.

Some apparent ambiguities may be resolved by careful attention to the problem actually under study. Consider the problem of evaluating some measure of total societal impact of risks in the production of iron in the United States, and note that perhaps one-third of the iron ore used is imported. Evidently some of the risk in producing iron ore comes from the risk of mining, milling, and transporting iron ore, but what risk measure should be assigned to imported iron ore to account for these risks in its production? There are at least three possibilities.

1. Assigning zero risk might be appropriate if the measure of risk required referred to the total risk of iron production to the population of the United States. Since import of iron ore causes no risk to any of the domestic population, any actual risks incurred in its production can be ignored. (Note that risk attribution to imports is not zero on a differential risk basis, because paying for the imports requires some actions that are not risk free.)

2. Assigning a risk measure equal to that incurred in production of ore in the United States is the simplest procedure and leads to indifference (from the point of view of total risk) between imports and domestic production. This assignment is equivalent to assuming that all variations in production occur in U.S. sources.

3. Assigning a risk measure equal to that actually incurred in overseas production is the most difficult option of the three because it requires much more analysis. It might be appropriate if the total risk of iron production to the global population were required.

In practice, the option usually chosen is (2), because the measure is available (it has to be computed in analysis of domestic production anyway), requires no decisions to be made on the domestic/import split (as would be required for (1)), and is an approximation to (3), if it may be assumed that risks are not too disparate between countries.

The position of system boundaries is of crucial concern also for risk comparisons between different systems (or projects, events, actions). For any use to be made of such comparisons, the systems under consideration should presumably be designed to perform similarly or to produce the same or similar results. An example that has attracted considerable attention recently (Inhaber 1979; Holdren et al. 1979; Crouch and Kline 1980) is the relative risks of systems for generating or converting energy, especially electricity, with special attention to comparisons between the so-called conventional systems (using coal, oil, gas, hydropower, or nuclear energy) and unconventional systems (such as various solar technologies, wind, biomass). Most of these technologies may be used for generating electricity, but comparison of the risks of different systems may be easily and grossly affected by alteration of system boundaries. The choice of system boundaries should, of course, be predicated on the exact question required to be answered in any such comparison. Some of the problems that must be faced are illustrated in the following list:

1. What risk measures are to be chosen? We have previously discussed this, but we note that it would be usual in this case to normalize to some unit size so as to get a risk per megawatt hour (MWh) generated, or per megawatt (MW) installed capacity, or per MW firm capacity (*firm* means available for use with some defined (high) probability). As before, choice of a particular measure or set of measures may not be straightforward.

2. Is total risk or incremental risk to be measured?

3. Should possible contributions to global effects be included or excluded? (Burning of fossil fuels contributes to carbon dioxide buildup in the atmosphere, which may lead to large-scale deleterious effects, but the best scientific opinions are currently divided as to the size and character of such effects.)

4. How are geographical siting factors to be taken into account? (Many of the "unconventional" systems produce results that would be strongly dependent on geographical siting: Wind systems require a windy environment; solar systems outputs vary with the availability of sunshine.)

5. Is the comparison to be made between typical systems, between averages taken over large numbers of systems or between marginal systems (the next to be built)? For the unconventional systems there is the problem that few, if any, have actually been built, so that unless care is exercised an attempt will be made to compare mature, optimized technologies with nonoptimized technologies. Whether this is of importance depends on what the risk comparison is supposed to show. Are such systems comparable from the point of view of the question to be answered?

6. Is the assessment supposed to be of systems with similar availability characteristics and, if so, what characteristics? (The *availability* of an electricity generating system measures the probability of it being able to produce electricity when it is called upon to do so.) Conventional electricity generating plants are designed to provide an availability high enough to supply power on demand. Solar and wind-powered electricity generating plants (for example) can provide output only during daylight and when the wind is blowing, respectively, unless they are backed up by other plants or by storage devices. If it is required to compare systems with high availability, then any solar system (for example) must include backup and/or storage, which should therefore be included within the system boundary. The amount of backup or storage will depend on the solar plant design, the availability requirements, and economic trade-offs. If no particular availability requirements are specified or if the load being supplied by the plant has the right characteristics, leading to availability requirements compatible with plant output availability, then no storage or backup systems need be included within the system boundaries.

The difference between the two cases (a whole spectrum of cases is possible) may be substantial, especially if any possible storage or backup devices prove to contribute large fractions of the measure of risk to the whole system, including the basic plant type. It is therefore essential that the system requirements be carefully specified in any comparisons between systems.

7. Should the system boundary be limited to the operating phase of the system, or should it include the construction, waste disposal, and fuel gathering? Further, should the total risk from all segments of the economy contributing to each of these phases be included or just the direct risks? Once again, the risks to include depend on the questions being answered. For the utility company, the relevant system boundary may be limited to direct construction risks, direct operation risks, and direct risks of waste disposal, whereas from a national viewpoint the boundary should, perhaps, be extended.

In Chapter 3 we will discuss in general terms how measures of risk such as these may in practice be evaluated. There may be other measures besides the few listed that are relevant in any given problem. It must be realized, however, that complete evaluation of all measures may not be possible because of lack of theoretical knowledge or lack of empirical data or even lack of time and furthermore that different opinions may be held on the extent of such lacks.

Some of the chain of events leading to harm to human beings may be known, but the whole causal chain, although strongly suspected, is incomplete. Consider the emission of toxic heavy metals in flue gases from burning fossil fuels. It is known that heavy metals are emitted, and estimates may be made of the quantities. It is also known that at high doses or dose rates such materials are toxic. But the doses or dose rates actually experienced by human beings from the emissions are usually much lower than those that elicit obvious toxic responses, and tests at the low doses or dose rates show results that are not statistically significant or are so subtle that there may be considerable argument over their reliability and meaning. Thus, although some effects at low doses may be strongly suspected, they must be considered practically unquantifiable, at least at present, so that their harm cannot be included in any direct measure of risk. In such cases the best that can be done is to quantify the relevant actions suspected of causing harm—in this case the emissions of heavy metals or the human exposure to such emissions—and use these quantities as surrogates for direct measures of risk to humans. Results of further research may ultimately allow conversion of the surrogate measures to direct measures of risk, but until then risk assessors will just have to note the surrogate measures together with any known resultant bounds on actual risk.

Complete evaluation of risk is also difficult in instances of differences of opinion on the existence of causal connections or on the magnitude of effects. As an extreme example, there are still persons who argue that the association of cigarette-smoking with lung cancer is not causal (that although there is an association between cigarette smoking and lung cancer, it is due to some other characteristic more common in both smokers and victims of lung cancer than in those who choose not to smoke or do not get lung cancer), so that, in their view, it is incorrect to attribute deaths due to lung cancer to cigarette smoking. The differences of opinion on magnitudes of effects can also be extreme. For many toxic materials it appears that there is a threshold dose below which acute toxic effects are not observed. For some types of toxic response (notably carcinogenesis, teratogenesis, mutagenesis), where there may be chronic effects even from single subacute doses, this observation may be unhelpful since even low doses might lead to delayed effects. Thus for small doses, some persons may suggest that there are no effects (threshold present), while others suggest substantial effects (no threshold present). The argument cannot be resolved by experiment, because testing on human beings is prevented on ethical grounds. Even if evidence on animals is acceptable, no test can disprove the existence of some response at low doses, because there is always a limit on the sensitivity of the test although experiment may set bounds on possible effects. Nor can the argument currently be resolved by theory, since sufficiently detailed theories are as yet unproved.

Although a complete theory about a certain risk may exist, lack of empirical data sometimes prevents complete evaluation of any particular measure of risk. Such lacks may arise in many ways, from budgetary considerations to discovery of new effects, where nobody ever collected the required data because nobody realized its relevance.

For some measures of risk, possibly those of greatest consequence in perceptions of risk, it is possible to make only a partially objective attempt at evaluation, because the measures themselves may be subjective or involve intangibles such as the quality of life. Measures including such variables as "days of pain" or distinguishing between different ways of dying necessarily are subjective in some degree.

Any evaluation of risk must be accompanied by a caveat on what is included or excluded. The caveat does not make the evaluation worthless, of course, for it is often possible to place bounds on the parts omitted. Perhaps more important, it ensures that the parts of any problem in which greatest uncertainty lies are exposed and separately brought to the attention of the analyst performing or using the risk assessment.

Suppose that, in accordance with the discussion so far, in conducting some risk assessment the measure or measures of risk have been agreed or the results shown insensitive to the choice, and furthermore that the boundaries of the task have been definitively drawn. Then although some major tasks have been performed, there are still further important considerations in using the values of measures of risk obtained from the evaluation methods of Chapter 3.

It is usual to find that the data used for evaluating risks have to be extrapolated in some way to cover the case of interest. Such extrapolation may be in time, geography, dose level, or size, and some model of the risk has to be constructed to perform the extrapolation. The necessity for extrapolation is illustrated by Figures 2-3 through 2-13, which show the variation over time of annual deaths and injuries per unit quantity of material mined in some of the mining industries. Applying such data to evaluate risks in a project that might take ten or more years to complete requires that the possibility of continued variation over time be included in the analysis. A possible model for some of the risks shown is to assume that these measures will continue to decrease exponentially; the cases where this gives reasonable fits to the available data are shown by the fitted lines on the figures and in Table 2-1, which shows the "halving times" for these cases. One should note the vertical error bars at several points on most of the graphs of death rates. These represent estimates of the statistical variability that may be expected in these rates due to the small numbers of deaths on which the rates are based.

In a similar manner, it may be necessary to construct models for extrapolation in other ways. Current actions can lead to events that pose risks in the future. Whether these risks are the same as those happening in the present from the same event may depend on circumstances that are not predictable but that have to be taken into account in any risk assessment. The same examples used before—carcinogenesis, teratogenesis, mutagenesis—serve as examples here. Exposure to various agents may result in cancers in twenty or more years, but whether the cancers will pose the same risk (of death or

Table 2-1.   Time for Risk Measures Graphed in Figures 2-3 to 2-13
to Halve in Those Cases for Which an Exponential Model is Applicable.

Material	Deaths	Injuries
Traprock	8.3	10.6
Limestone and dolomite	N.A.	9.5
Coal		
(1950–76)	10.2	N.A.
(1940–76)	10.3	N.A.
Lime	8.3	N.A.
Granite	7.4	7.3
Cement	7.7	N.A.
Copper	14.3	11.9
Iron ore	11.4	36.4 (1956–71)
Lead and zinc	19.2	15.0

N.A.: Not Applicable.

suffering) then is moot, for cure rates may have improved. Similarly disposal of carcinogenic waste materials now may lead to exposure after hundreds of thousands of years or more, at which time it is possible that all cancers might be preventable or curable.

Extrapolations from available data necessarily lead to uncertainty of at least two kinds in the evaluation of risk. The first and easiest to treat is statistical uncertainty in estimating the measure of risk from the data or in estimating the extrapolation model parameters. Given the model, however, it is relatively straightforward to evaluate statistical confidence limits to be placed on any estimates of risks.

The source of the second kind of uncertainty, which is much less tractable to analysis but often greater in magnitude than the first, lies in the choice of model. In some cases, where every link in the chain of causality has been investigated, there may be little choice, for it is "known" upon what variables the risks depend. In other cases this definiteness is not available and it is up to investigators to make their own best choice. The graphs given earlier illustrate this; there is no known theory to explain how many deaths will occur in mining. We have assumed that the annual number of deaths correlates with the quantity of material mined, and we show how this correlation varies with time. If we project the trends shown on the graphs into the future, we are adopting a model that says that the annual number of

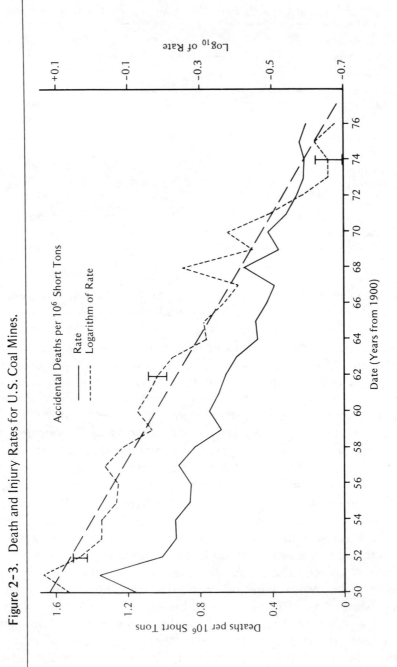

Figure 2-3.   Death and Injury Rates for U.S. Coal Mines.

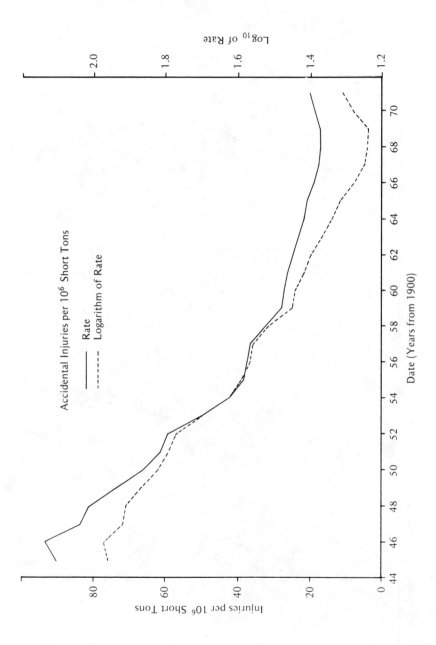

Figure 2-4. Death and Injury Rates for U.S. Cement Quarries and Mills.

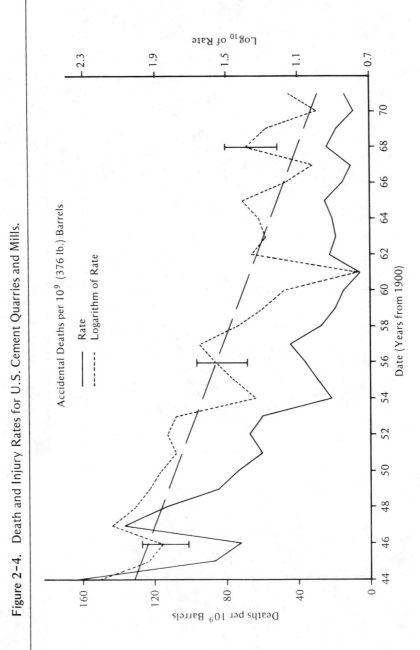

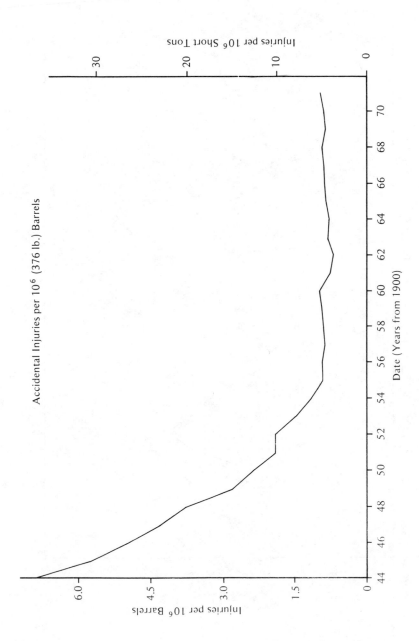

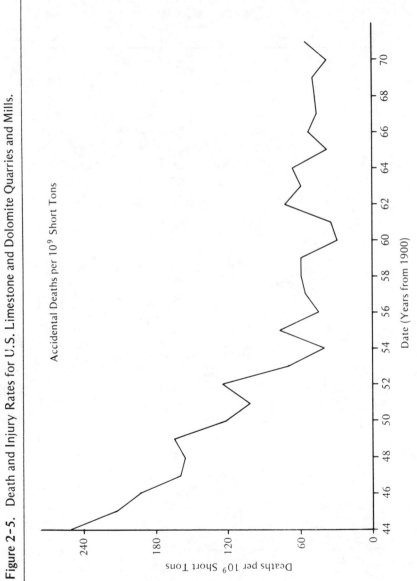

Figure 2-5.   Death and Injury Rates for U.S. Limestone and Dolomite Quarries and Mills.

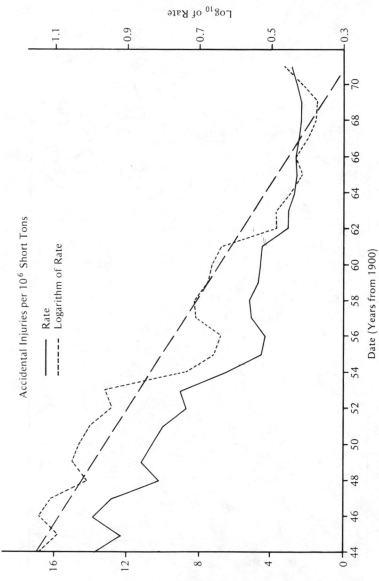

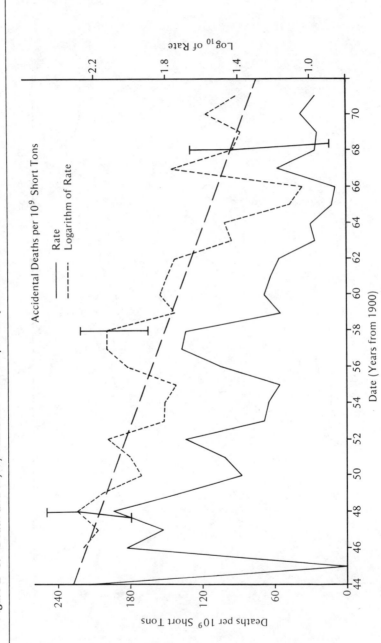

Figure 2-6. Death and Injury Rates for U.S. Traprock Quarries and Mills.

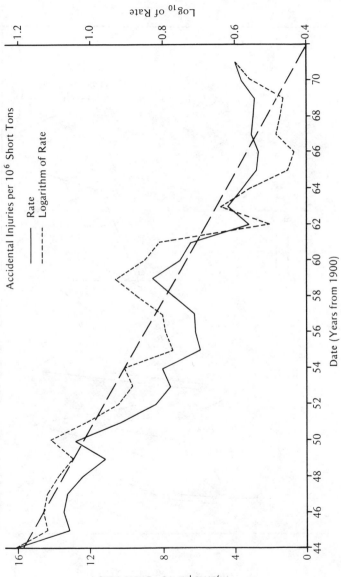

Accidental Injuries per 10^6 Short Tons

—— Rate
------ Logarithm of Rate

Log_{10} of Rate

Injuries per 10^6 Short Tons

Date (Years from 1900)

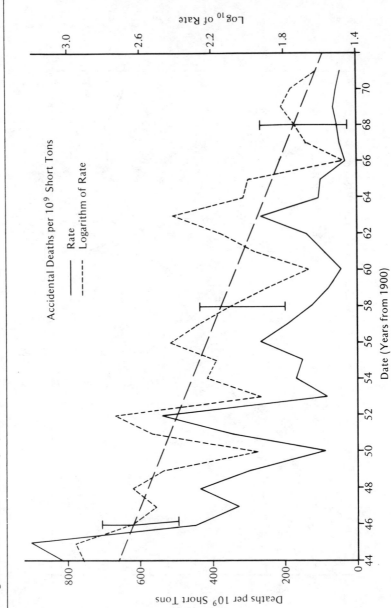

Figure 2-7. Death and Injury Rates for U.S. Granite Mining.

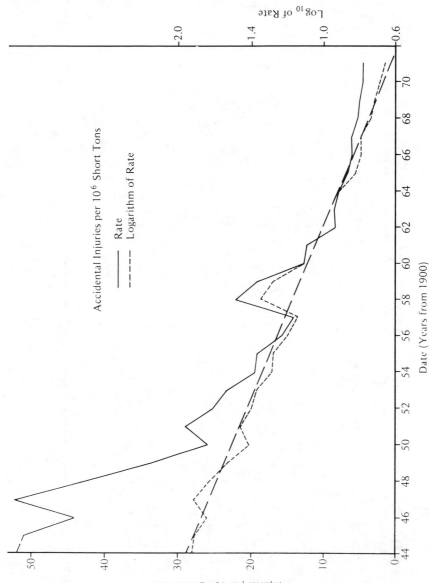

Figure 2-8.   Death and Injury Rates for U.S. Sand and Gravel Plants.

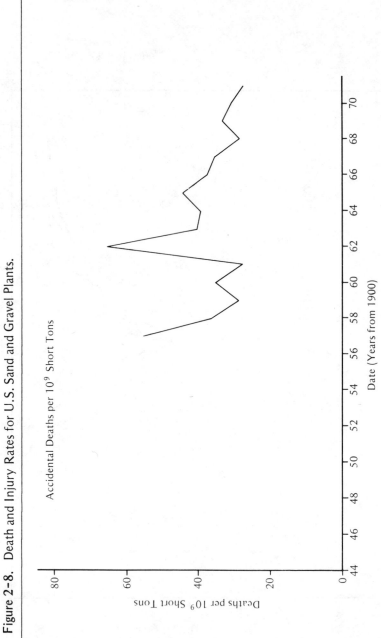

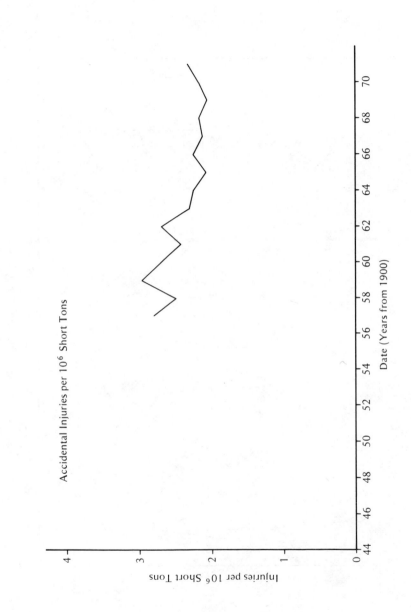

Accidental Injuries per 10⁶ Short Tons

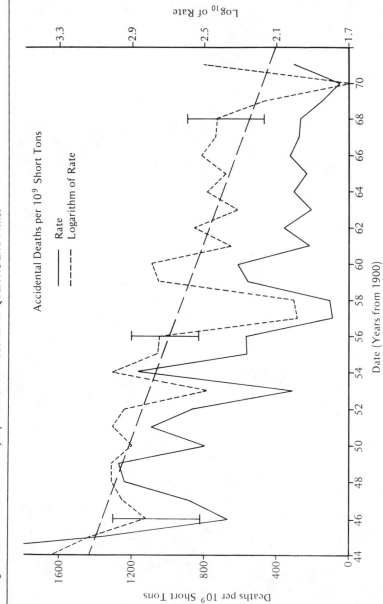

Figure 2-9.   Death and Injury Rates for U.S. Lime Quarries and Mills.

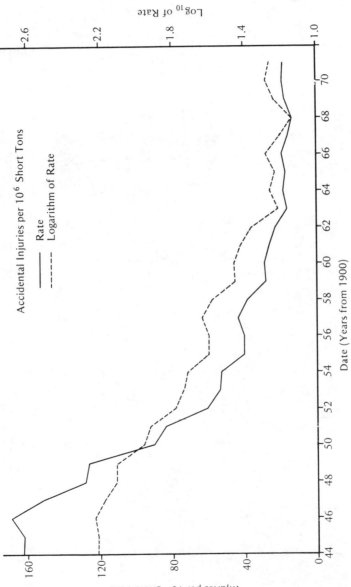

Figure 2-10. Death and Injury Rates for U.S. Iron Ore Mines.

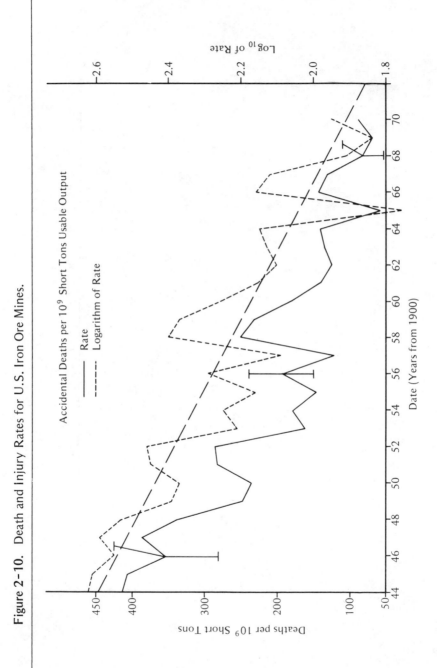

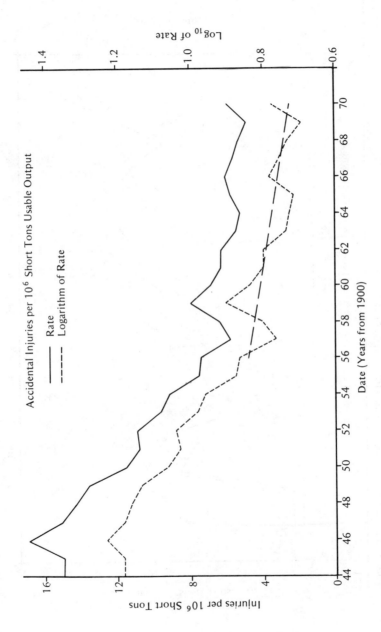

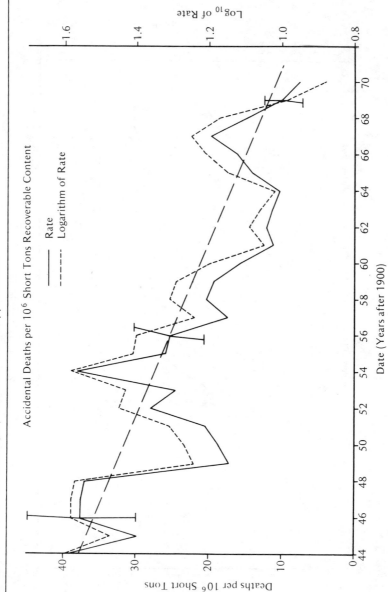

Figure 2-11. Death and Injury Rates for U.S. Copper Mines.

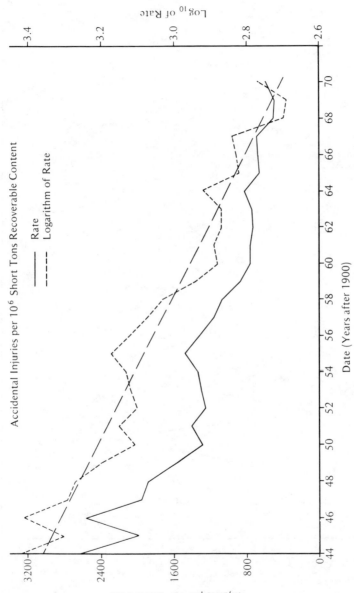

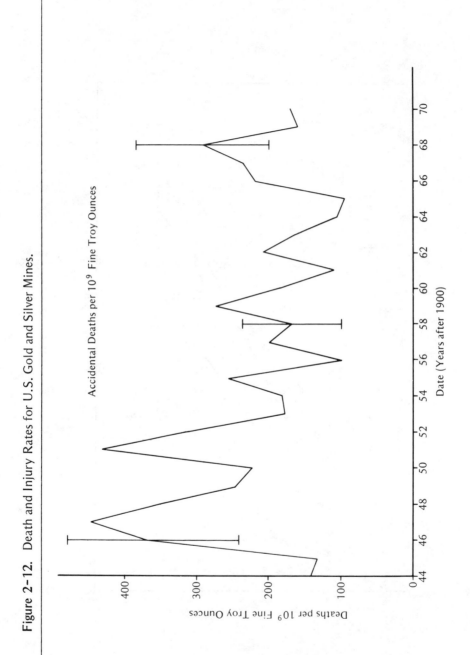

Figure 2–12.   Death and Injury Rates for U.S. Gold and Silver Mines.

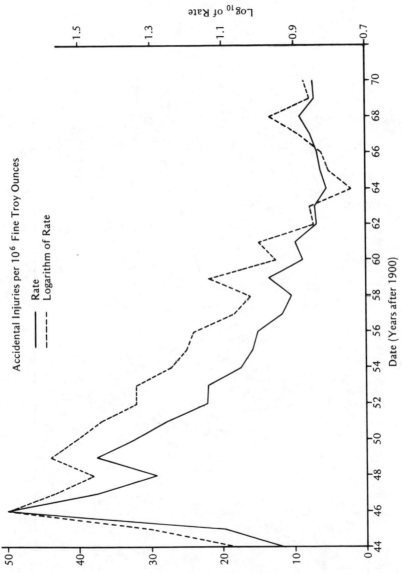

Figure 2–13. Death and Injury Rates for U.S. Lead and Zinc Mines.

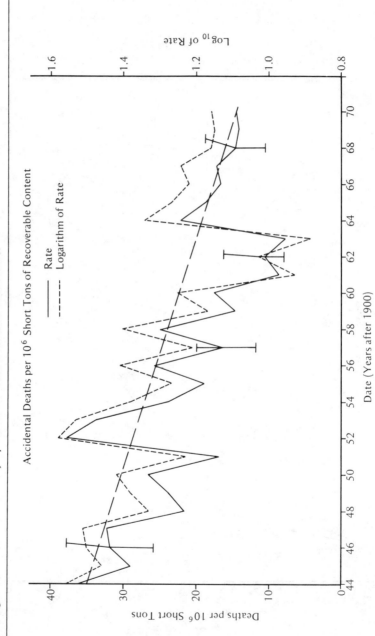

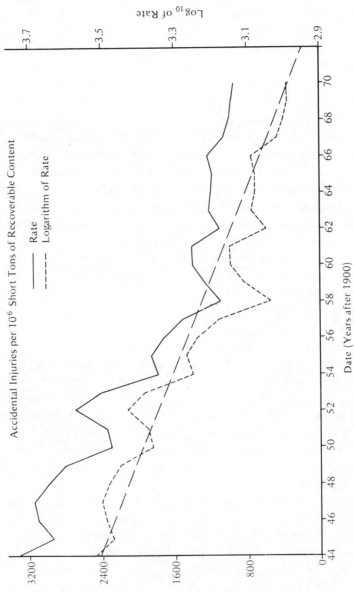

deaths is proportional to the amount mined, with a proportionality constant varying with time in the manner in which we make the projection. It is possible, however, that the annual number of deaths is not proportional to the amount of material mined. Instead it may be that both these variables depend in such a way on other variables (such as manhours worked, number of miners, ages of miners) that in the past the time variation of their ratio has varied as shown on the figures. In this case the future variation of this measure need bear no relation to how it has varied in the past, so past trends may give no indication of future trends.

The uncertainty associated with such model errors may be very large and may easily exceed any purely statistical errors. One way of estimating such uncertainties would be to evaluate the effects of using different, but still plausible, models. Usually, uncertainty increases with the distance of extrapolation, where *distance* is some measure of the departure from the conditions under which the data were measured. It should also be borne in mind that, in cases where there is uncertainty over the model, any consensus that exists should not be taken to indicate that the consensus model is correct, although in some cases of risk assessment such a consensus model would be the right one to use so long as any results included the caveat that that model had been used.

The uncertainties and caveats attached to any risk estimate are as important (if not more important) than the risk estimate itself and should always be included in any use of the risk estimate. These components indicate the areas where the greatest lack of knowledge is concentrated or the areas where human judgment must be applied. For use in risk/cost/benefit analysis, such areas are exactly those that must be closely studied and are almost the only ones where analysts have to exercise their skills. Anything that is certain can be handled automatically.

We have attempted to define the meaning of risk by discussing risk analysis. Readers may have noticed how firmly we hold the opinion that risk analysis, and more generally, risk/cost/benefit analysis, cannot properly be performed without close attention to the decision at issue. The risk analyst is not the decisionmaker, however, so the risk analyst should attempt to work objectively while remembering that the decisionmaker cannot use any parts of the analysis which appear irrelevant. Risk analysis may be considered as a branch of decision analysis, on which there are now some good references available. But there are crucial distinctions in practice. In the usual domain of decision analysis, business, choice is between options that differ only slightly, with consequences varying by perhaps 30 percent, the difference between bankruptcy and a comfortable profit margin. Catastrophes need never be explicitly considered in any business decision because society takes care, at least to some extent, of the consequences of catastrophe by its bankruptcy laws. Decisions are usually required on short-term problems.

Risk/benefit analysis, on the other hand, is called upon to deal with decisions involving much greater uncertainty, where catastrophes have to be explicitly considered and may contribute substantially to both uncertainty and expected values, and the problems may be very long term. In cases of large uncertainties, one use of risk analysis may be to set bounds on the possible consequences of decisions, and these bounds may then be used in the risk/cost/benefit analysis as some form of worst expected case.

REFERENCES

Crouch, E., and R. Kline. 1980. "An Analysis of Two Reports on Risk Assessment." Unpublished report, Energy and Environmental Policy Center, Harvard University.

Holdren, J.P.; K. Anderson; P.H. Gleick; I. Mintzer; G. Morris; and K.R. Smith. 1979. "Risk of Renewable Energy Sources: A Critique of the Inhaber Report." Unpublished paper ERG 79-3, Energy and Resources Group, University of California.

Inhaber, H. 1979. "Risk of Energy Production." Unpublished report AECB 1119, Atomic Energy Control Board, Ottawa.

3 ESTIMATION OF RISK

Once the risk analyst has decided which risk measures to use and within which system boundaries to use them, there comes the task of estimating the magnitude of the measures. This task must be borne in mind while considering the problems in Chapter 2, because the available methods and data affect what analysis is possible. The task is to obtain a numerical result for both the size of the risk measure and its uncertainty, or equivalent information.

The methods to be adopted depend to a large extent on the nature of the risk and on the adverse consequences of the events constituting the risk. Different methods may be appropriate depending on the past occurrences of the risky events or similar ones; their frequency of occurrence, either expected or observed; their size and severity; and on predictions or expectations for risks that have not previously occurred or have not been observed.

We will distinguish between two classes of risks, "historical" and "new." Historical risks are those in which the adverse events associated with them have occurred (and may continue to occur) often enough for data sufficient for analysis to have been accumulated. Often such risks have aroused some interest, so that some theory or model exists that is sufficiently detailed to allow useful conclusions about the magnitude of the risk. Examples of historical risks include the risks of or from diseases, motor vehicles, industrial accidents, pollution, weather phenomena (hurricanes, tornadoes, lightning).

Some risks are historical in the sense that some event has happened in the past that could happen again and would produce adverse consequences if it did. If the frequency of occurrence is too low, insufficient data will be accumulated to allow use of the methods common for more frequent historical risks. In such cases, it may be better to proceed as for new risks.

New risks consist of those arising from events never previously observed although they may have happened without being observed. In many cases some sort of risk may be expected by analogy with historic experience (for example, exposure to various organic chemicals may be expected to pose some risk), or it may be possible to predict theoretically the possibility of an adverse event (say, ignition of the cloud of methane gas released following a collision of a tanker carrying liquified natural gas), even though the event has never occurred. New risks range from catastrophic but improbable events (meteor impacts, dam breaks, reactor meltdowns) to highly probable, low-consequence events (such as risks arising from exposure to new chemicals). The methods of evaluation may appear to differ for such disparate classes of risk, but the difference is largely in the different emphasis placed on the different parts of the analysis. The basic idea is to break down any new risk into a sequence of events, each of which may be analyzed separately by theory, by analogy with historical risks or from actual occurrence, and then to reconstruct the whole from these parts.

Before considering the methods used for evaluation of historical and new risks, it is necessary to realize that all such evaluations of risk depend on a model or theory of how the risk is incurred. Even statements about the magnitude of any given measure of risk in the past usually assume either implicitly or explicitly some model or theory. (Examples in Chapter 3 quoted an annual probability of death per ton of material mined with the implicit assumption of a causal correlation between the quantity mined and the probability of death.) In this application, we make no distinction between a model and a theory, each being a description often in mathematical terms of how something (such as magnitude of risk measure) will change when some "external" variables (such as date, quantity of material, number of manhours, size of plant) change.

In applications it is usually necessary to make some sort of extrapolation in order to obtain risk measures relevant to the problem at hand. That is, given a model describing how the risk depends on various variables, it is usually necessary to estimate the risk for a set of values of the variables not included in the data used to establish the model. Perhaps the commonest such variable is time. Many data on past events may allow estimation of some risk in the past, but to make predictions about the future the variable *time* must be changed in the model. Of course, if the risks do not vary with time in the model, changing this variable will not alter the risk estimate. Other common examples include the variables of size, dose, or concentration. Thus data might be obtained on the risk of death or injury in an American industry as a function of the size of the establishment, permitting conception of a model with size of establishment as a variable. The model would then be "fitted to the data"—that is, the model would be chosen so that it reproduced the data as closely as possible—and might then be used to estimate risks in an establishment size not included in the initial data by changing the variable *size of establishment* in the model.

The model or theory used may actually correspond to "the way things really are"—that is, it may correspond to the real physical world in some sense. The best verified theories do correspond to the physical world, at least over a restricted range of values of the variables. Such theories include the so-called laws of physics, many of which, in the form known to and used by nonspecialists, are applicable only in restricted ranges of variables. (They are usually approximations to more general "laws" valid over a much wider range of variables.) Thus, the usual notion of addition of velocities applies only for velocities small compared with that of light; Newton's law of gravity applies only if the gravitational fields are not too large; classical mechanics is an excellent approximation only for objects that are not too small. Physical laws serve as examples here because they have usually been the best verified, but it is necessary to point out that all such laws are simply a codification of observations about the physical world. They may be used for prediction within the range of variables for which they are good approximations, but for extrapolation outside such ranges they may give incorrect results and require modification. In the cases mentioned, the ranges of variables for which they are good approximations includes almost all the cases likely to be met in everyday situations.

The best theories tend to be those in which causal connections have been established between different events—cause and effect (by *best theories* and *established* we mean those that give consistently accurate predictions and are thus widely accepted as valid). The physical laws mentioned fall into this category. On the other hand there are many cases in which no direct connection is apparent, but there are indications that one may exist. There is usually observed, for example, a statistical relation between the size of establishments in a given industry and the injury and accident rate for employees working in the establishment. The correlation between establishment size and injury rate is unlikely to be directly causal although it is easy to hypothesize about the exact relation between establishment size and the direct causes. Using the correlation as a predictive tool may be an acceptable theory for estimating injury rates; for a given industry, if a stable relation between establishment size and injury rate has been observed in the past, it may be acceptable to estimate future injury rates as a function of establishment size on the basis of this relation.

One can postulate an indirect linking between the variable of the theory (size of establishment) and effect (injury rate); for example, larger establishments may be required to employ safety officers, the actions of whom may reduce injury rates; or contrariwise, smaller establishments may be loath to take on more dangerous jobs. It is possible to use a "theory" in which it is known that no causal connection exists but merely a correlation. In the analysis of the effects of air pollution on human health, it is not known which component(s) of the pollution actually cause health effects at the low doses encountered, so it is not certain that the "effects" are actually caused by the component of pollution that is measured (typical measures are levels of sulfur oxides, nitrogen oxides, hydrocarbons, ozone, opacity of the air, total suspended particulates). However, since the different components tend to be generated together, it is reasonable to assume (and for those components so far measured the assumption turns out to be reasonably valid) that all the components vary together—their levels are highly correlated—so that measurement of one or several gives an indirect measure of all the others. The theory so constructed, in which health effects are related to the levels of measured pollutants, may then give valid predictions provided the proxy variable used (level of pollutant actually measured) maintains the same relation (correlation) to the actual harmful pollution constituent. It should be noticed that the previous example, size of establishment versus injury rates, may also be an example of the last type.

The use of proxy variables in theories or models is common in risk assessment, where the variables controlling the magnitude of risks are often not known or not quantifiable (involving many human factors) or so complex as to defy useful analysis. In such cases it is usual to use plausible proxy variables in a theory constructed to fit whatever data are available. Generally the simplest model that fits the data and that permits sensible extrapolation of the required amount is the most useful and believable, Occam's razor being a useful tool to master. But the use of proxy variables can be extremely dangerous; spurious results can be obtained if an important confounding variable is omitted. The death rate in the United States is correlated with air pollution variables, but whether this is a causal correlation or not is a matter still in dispute. It is possible that the true causal connection is with some combination of, for example, cigarette smoking, occupation, and income level.

The use of a parametric model, as described, allows a numerical estimation of the magnitude of a measure of risk, and also an estimation of the uncertainty in that numerical value. When comparing such numerical values (examples are given in Chapter 7) it is necessary to give some thought to their interpretation, for the interpretation may vary depending on the context. In most cases, any such figures will be averages over geographical regions, over populations, over time, over other variables used in the models. Suppose, for example, we have estimates of the magnitudes of the annual probability of death from various events for the whole population of the United States. Although such estimates give an accurate picture of total annual deaths in the United States, they may be wildly inaccurate if applied to any particular subgroup of the nation's population or to any particular individual. This is easy to see if one considers just the risk of dying from any cause. An average over the whole American population may be obtained from the average death rate, which is about 9×10^{-3} per year (about 1.9 million people die per year out of a population of about 210 million), but for the subgroup consisting of males over the age of eighty-five the risk of dying was about 0.18 per year in 1975, substantially higher. For any such subgroup an estimate of the risk can be obtained by averaging over just that subgroup (as was done to obtain the figure 0.18 in the last sentence), but again this figure cannot be accurately applied to any specific member of the subgroup, unless all that is known about that specific person is that he is a member of the subgroup.

Another sort of averaging, over long time spans, should be borne in mind when considering certain other risks. There is a class of events that could have annual average risks just as large as the everyday causes of death but that do not result in deaths occurring every year. These are events that are very unusual (average number less than one per year) but that may have very large consequences when they do occur. (If they are both unusual and have small consequences, we are not so interested in them.) Examples of such infrequent and possibly large-consequence events are earthquakes, dam bursts, and meteor strikes. This varied amount and varied type of averaging creates problems for comparison of risks, because even when put on an apparently equivalent scale (like annual average), equal risks on that scale may be very different. An extreme example of this problem is to compare the case of automobile accidents (probability of death $\sim 2 \times 10^{-4}$ per year, resulting in $\sim 45,000$ deaths per year in the United States) with a hypothetical event occurring with probability 2×10^{-4} per year (once every 5,000 years on average) but killing almost everybody in the United States. The average annual risk is the same, but it seems unlikely that these two risks should be considered equivalent.

Bearing in mind the foregoing discussion, we now turn to the classification of risks, starting with those labeled *historical.* Such risks usually arise from events of comparatively high probability, so that an appreciable number occur annually in the population at risk, but of comparatively low consequence (fewer than about ten deaths per event). (We can omit high-probability, high-consequence events, since society has developed in such a way as to eliminate them—that is, no such events exist—the consequences of high-probability events have been reduced or the occurrence rate of high-consequence events has been reduced.) The meaning of *comparatively high probability* varies with context. For example, an event occurring to an individual with average probability of 10^{-5} per year, which would be considered a rare event individually (fewer than 1 in 1,000 people would experience it in a lifetime), corresponds to a high-probability event in the context of the whole American population of more than 200 million people (since it would occur annually about $10^{-5} \times 2 \times 10^{8}$ = 2,000 times per year). Thus we can have a risk that an individual perceives to be small and will take no action to avoid but that society might perceive to be large and spend considerable resources on reducing.

The large number of events occurring gives a good data base for testing and fitting models, and it is usually sufficient to use the simplest model that fits the data and is physically reasonable for the extrapolations envisaged. It is unnecessary to have a detailed theory on why the event occurs, unless one is interested in estimating the changes in the risk following various specific actions. This method can be applied to accidents (traffic, mountain climbing, drowning) and many natural hazards (rain, flood, snow, hail, lightning, and the incidence of some diseases). For such cases we might assume that the future probability of an event is equal to the past probability and the consequences of any event similar in the future to those in the past. Alternatively, any time trends observed may be incorporated as approximations to the complicated set of changes in conditions that actually may occur.

A simple case of such a trend might be steady change in the number of potential accident initiators (say, automobiles) or a steady change in conditions affecting the risk (a steady improvement in the safety of automobiles). Despite the possibility of such changes in the future, the uncertainty of the risk estimates is comparatively small, because the mechanisms causing risks are many or unalterable either in practice or in theory even though the mechanisms may be unknown. Figure 3–1 shows that despite the year-to-year variation, the risk of death in an automobile accident has stayed in the range 21–28 per 10^5 persons per year over 25 years so that we can be fairly confident that the rate will, ceteris paribus, be (2.4×10^{-4}) ± 10 percent for several years more. Figure 3–1 also shows that the death rate per vehicle or per vehicle mile has a smoother trend, so that a model that assumes the number of traffic fatalities proportional to vehicle miles traveled or number of cars may give a more accurate estimate of the risk expressed as the death rate per vehicle mile or per car. Of course, if the risk measure of interest were the death rate per 10^5 population, estimates of vehicle miles traveled or number of cars would also be required.

The procedure outlined can often be used to give an estimate for the risk of some consequence among some subsection of the population, (say, the risk of death from pneumoconiosis, better known as black lung disease, among miners), even though the causal relation between action and consequence is less obvious. This can be done because the subsection differs from the general population. Next it is logical to ask why this difference occurs and what measures may be

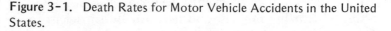

Figure 3-1.   Death Rates for Motor Vehicle Accidents in the United States.

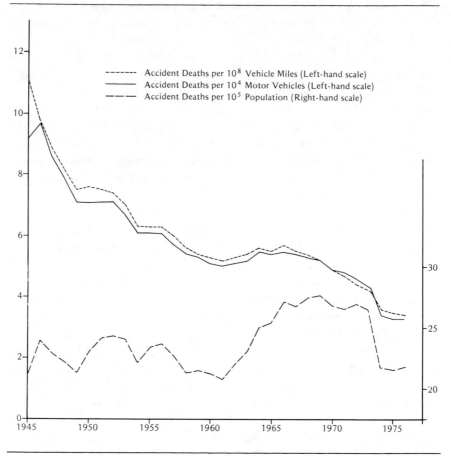

taken to reduce the higher risk. In the case mentioned, further study indicates that the risk of pneumoconiosis depends in some way on the amount of dust inhaled, allowing an analysis to define this dependence quantitatively. The risk can then be assigned to a particular cause, inhalation of dust, rather than to the more general and less useful heading, coal mining. In other cases there may be a lot of historical data on consequences, especially mortality and morbidity, leading to the suspicion that some action is causing at least some of the consequences, but there may be no clear subgroups among the population that differ only in their exposure to that action. A good example is general air pollution, which is suspected to cause an in-

crease in mortality and morbidity. Many studies have shown correlations between some measures of air pollution and mortality and
morbidity, but a correlation is insufficient to prove causality, since
there are many other variables (often called *confounding variables* —
income level, smoking habits, occupation, geographical location)
that are or may be correlated with both. The most complete analyses
of mortality, attempting to account for as many such other variables
as possible, still show some effect from air pollution, so that to it can
be ascribed a yearly risk of 2.5×10^{-4} averaged over the United
States. The uncertainty in this estimate is large (± 100 percent), for
without evidence of direct cause and effect the effects suspected to
be caused by air pollution may in fact be caused by some other variable that has been missed in the analysis; laboratory evidence shows
acute morbid effects for air pollution, but only at levels substantially
higher than observed in American cities, although of course this does
not exclude a chronic effect on mortality.

Specializing to the cancer risk from air pollution allows greater
certainty. Various polycyclic aromatic hydrocarbons are produced in
combustion processes, and one of them, benzo(α)pyrene (BαP) is
widely measured and is used as a surrogate for the others. At high
concentrations of BαP, as breathed by coke oven workers and roof-
ers, the lung cancer rate is large enough to be observable and causality can be established. If we assume proportionality with dose, we
find a total cancer rate in the United States of 3,000/year from this
cause, a risk of 1.5×10^{-5} /year.

The preceding examples illustrate the general rule that, even if
there is copious historical data, no risk estimate may be extrapolated
into the future without assuming some sort of theoretical model. The
air pollution example indicates that even past risks may be uncertain
lacking a sure theoretical framework. Unless there is good reason for
any alternative, Occam's razor indicates that the simplest theory that
well explains the data should be used, so that in cases where the
cause–effect relation is not well understood the best predictor of
future risk is whichever specific risk appears to have the smoothest
trend in the past. Thus in the automobile example, the number of
vehicles or the number of vehicle miles traveled appear to be more
closely related to the death rate than does the total population, so
that the number of deaths per automobile or the number of deaths
per vehicle mile gives less uncertainty in the risk estimates than does
the number of deaths per capita. A similar situation obtains in the

coal mining industry (Figures 2-1 and 2-2), where it appears that the death rate per ton of coal mined has a smoother time trend than either the death rate per man hour or per person employed, so that the amount of coal mined is a better predictor of the total number killed than are manhours worked or persons employed.

Using this method consists basically of adjusting some physically reasonable model to fit past data and then extrapolating from it to new situations. Associated with each risk estimate made this way will be an uncertainty, which must be evaluated in order to know how much confidence can be placed in the estimate of risk. Uncertainty arises from two basic sources. The most difficult to deal with is error in the choice of model—that is, choosing a model or theory that is not in accord with physical reality and thus may give incorrect predictions. The other uncertainty is due to statistical variations and is much simpler.

In most risk estimates, the measure of risk estimated is not a definite quantity but incorporates in some way a set of probabilities. Usually what is required is an expected value, or mean value, of the risk measure. We can illustrate with a hypothetical example: Suppose every year every member of the population played Russian roulette just once, with one bullet in a six-chambered gun. The annual risk of death from Russian roulette in that population would be 1/6; that is, on average, one-sixth the population would be killed each year. But we would not expect exactly one-sixth of the population to die each year; the actual number in any year could be from none to all. The expected value is 1/6, but in any given year we expect some deviation from 1/6. This variation corresponds to the statistical uncertainty of the estimate, and some measure of the variation must be appended to the estimate. In most cases, the model chosen incorporates such statistical uncertainty, not only predicting an expected value but also giving an uncertainty estimate, although all too often risk analysts quote only the expected value.

Unfortunately, life is not quite as simple as the foregoing discussion makes it appear. Because of the variability of real life, the data used to construct the model contain some deviations from the expected values, so that the fit of the model to such data is almost invariably slightly wrong, so that the values predicted by the model are also wrong in both expected value and uncertainty estimate. This effect is, however, relatively straightforward to allow for using statistical techniques, the result being an increase in the size of the uncertainty.

The more difficult problem is to try and estimate the uncertainty caused by the possible choice of an erroneous model. The likelihood that any estimates suffer from this type of error depends on the case being considered and the theories being used—on how well they have been tested and how applicable they are. The model may fit very well to any existing data and give extrapolated estimates with small statistical error estimates, which are nevertheless many times further from the real world values than would be expected from such statistical error estimates. There is no general technique for estimating this sort of error, but certain methods sometimes can give an idea of their magnitude, although quantitative statements are difficult to make.

These methods can be summarized as "choosing worst (or best) cases." Different models are tried, adjusted to fit the available data as well as possible, and then examined to assess what they predict in the required situation. The different models may be variations on a single theme, obtained, for example, by varying some parameters within the original model, or they may be widely disparate in underlying philosophy. The only requirements are plausibility and consistency with available data. Consistency should be extended to include relevant other cases where data are available; the test of plausibility is necessarily dependent on opinion. If any consensus can be reached on best and worst estimates, then some measure of uncertainty is represented, but it must be recognized that no quantitative statements can be made about such estimates, for they are statements of belief.

The ideas just presented can perhaps be clarified by means of a specific example, the risk of death in the United States from extreme weather conditions (tornadoes, floods, hurricanes, lightning). Data of reasonable reliability on extreme weather phenomena exist for some time in the historic past; plots of annual numbers of deaths against time are shown in Figure 3–2. Over long periods (tens to hundreds of years the weather is expected to be reasonably constant, but year-to-year variations in extreme weather conditions are large. Thus a value can be given for the expected risk of death, but any model used must include large year-to-year variability. The simplest model to adopt appears to be one in which some measure of the mean value of the risk is constant or perhaps changing slowly with time. Adopting this

Figure 3-2. Death Rates for Tornadoes, Floods, and Cyclones in the United States.

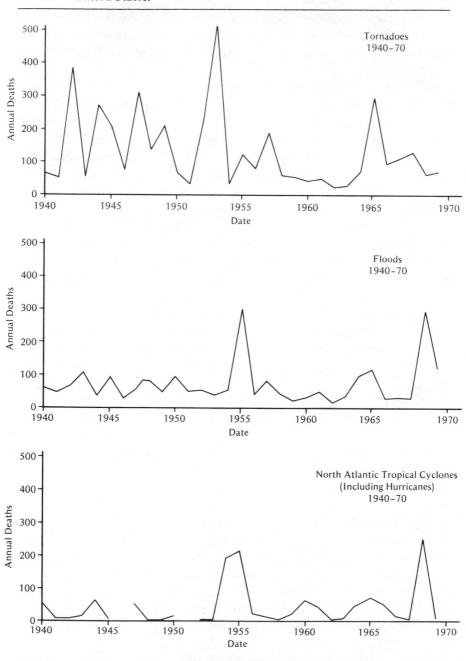

Source: U.S. Bureau of the Census (1975).

model does not mean explicitly including causal effects, but it is hoped that the risks are so many or unalterable (in the short term) that the model is effectively causal without the causal chains being known in detail. Randomness is used to advantage in this case to estimate mean values that are reasonably constant or slowly varying, despite the great variations within each possible causal chain. For example, for the subcase of people being killed by blown projectiles, the probability of a death involves a complicated product of the number of available projectiles, the population density, the probability of people not taking shelter, and other factors. There are very large numbers of people and events and a small probability of any particular event causing harm to any particular person; an average is taken over the many possibilities, not all of which are likely to be simultaneously affected by changes. If there are cases in which changes may affect all possibilities, the changes may be taken into account. A good example is injuries from tornadoes, for which warnings and advice on what to do have improved in the historic past and may be expected to continue to improve; the reduction of injuries caused by tornadoes has been ascribed to the improved information about them.

We previously mentioned the history of deaths from automobile accidents in the United States, adopting a model that simply assumed constant or decreasing annual risk of death per person or per vehicle mile. Sufficient data are available to introduce more complex models in this case. It would be possible to take into account different risks for highway versus urban driving or driving on freeways versus city streets and to include factors such as alcohol consumption. Whether such breakdowns would be of any use for predictions of the future would depend on the availability and reliability of estimates of the future behavior of such variables.

So far we have discussed the historical risks, those of high probability but low consequence for which there is a good historic record. For other risks, *new* in our nomenclature, no direct historic record is available or applicable. Such risks include those of low probability but large consequence, together with unprecedented ones of both high and low probability and consequence, usually due to the changing nature of society and its actions. It is possible that there is indirect historic evidence available on certain new risks, for there may be evidence available on similar risks or there may be data on investigations that found no evidence of risk.

Note that lack of evidence should not be confused with evidence of lack. If an investigation finds no evidence of risk, it does not follow necessarily that the risk is zero, since the investigation may have been insensitive and thus unable to distinguish between zero and a small positive effect. Thus, for example, the fact that epidemiological studies of human beings have found no compelling evidence of a carcinogenic effect from saccharin consumption does not prove no risk exists. It does show that, if there is such an effect, it is probably less than the smallest effect that could have been detected by those epidemiological studies.

In order to make estimates of the magnitude of new risks, it is necessary to relate them in some way to historic data, meaning that some model (that is, theory) must be adopted that allows the extrapolation from historic cases to the new situation. This may be done by analogy with similar historic cases. Thus people generally attempt to assess the risks of new toxic materials by analogy with materials known from long experience to be toxic, expecting to find "threshold" exposures that lead to immediate toxic effects such as death, and some form of relation between dose, measured in some way, and chronic response or long-term effects. Ethically, dose-response relations cannot be deliberately evaluated in human subjects, so they must be evaluated ab initio by theory (from detailed knowledge of the way the body reacts to the chemicals—currently not possible), or from in vitro or in vivo testing of animals. Consider the problem of evaluating carcinogenic risks from chemicals as an example of the methods used for estimating human response from animal and other data. (For a complete risk assessment, it would also be necessary to know the human exposure to the chemical).

It would of course be desirable to have a complete theory of carcinogenesis, so that the risk of a chemical could be calculated from first principles. Although theories are being worked on (Cairns 1978), it is not practical to wait for their development before making decisions about the use of chemicals, so that we must use what information we do have to the best of our ability. We already have sufficient knowledge derived from past experience with other carcinogens in man and animals to provide useful estimates of the magnitude of the cancer risk from any chemical, if certain tests have been performed on the chemical.

The experiments performed currently are in vitro mutagenesis tests of various kinds, and lifetime tests for carcinogenesis on laboratory animals, usually rats and mice. The problem occurs in using the results of these experiments to predict the response of humans. It has long been regarded as prudent to assume that an animal carcinogen is also a human carcinogen, but there are theoretical arguments over the validity of using quantitative comparisons because of the differences in metabolism between the various species. However, results now exist from large numbers of experiments performed under relatively standard conditions, so that it is possible to attempt empirical, quantitative comparisons. For many, but not all chemicals there is a close relation between the potency of a chemical in in vitro mutagenesis tests and in animal carcinogenesis tests. This was shown, for example, by Meselson and Russell (1977) (see Figure 3-3). Results also are being accumulated from many carcinogenesis bioassays performed on rats and mice for the National Cancer Institute, using a standard protocol. The animals are administered various doses of the chemical being tested (up to the maximum they can tolerate) and watched for their whole lifetime. By assuming that the cancer risk is proportional to the daily dose received (measured as a fraction of the body weight), we have been able to demonstrate a high correlation of carcinogenic potency between the rat and mouse species used, over a range of 10^4 in potency. A chemical that is a potent carcinogen in one species is also potent in the other, and given the potency in one species it can be estimated to within a factor of about 10 in the other (see Figure 3-4). This suggests that the animal data and possibly, eventually, the in vitro mutagenesis data can be used to predict the risk to man for any chemical tested. We have attempted to make a similar comparison of potencies between animals and man (Crouch and Wilson 1979) (see Figure 3-5), in those few cases where we have some information, albeit poor, on the effects in both animals and man. The lack of standardized experiments and the poor quality of the data would be expected to lead to a much larger amount of variability in our results in these cases, but nevertheless one can see that the potency in man is predicted (within a factor of 10) by the largest measured potency among the animals. Risk to human beings can thus be related to the quantity of chemical absorbed. It is important to realize that the assumption that the cancer incidence is proportional to dose is not proved or denied by experiment. It is a conservative assumption in the sense that few people seriously propose anything more pessimistic (that is, it is difficult to produce plausible theories that produce more pessimistic effects).

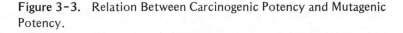

Figure 3-3.   Relation Between Carcinogenic Potency and Mutagenic Potency.

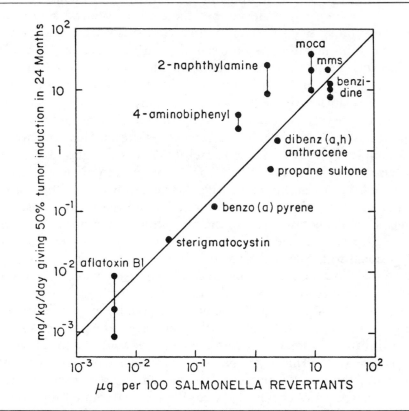

Source: Meselson and Russell (1977).

Although some new risks are amenable to techniques similar to those described, where everything is done all at once, as it were, this is not possible for all cases. With some limited experience, statistical techniques can be used, together with a highly simplified theory, to derive bounds on probabilities of occurrence of some of the events constituting the risk. As an example, consider the loss of coolant accident (LOCA) in pressurized light water nuclear reactors (PWR). Besides estimation of the probability of this accident by other means, there has been considerable experience in running such nuclear reactors (400 reactor years worldwide) in which time one LOCA has occurred. Assuming that a LOCA is equally likely to occur in any

Figure 3-4. Relation Between Carcinogenic Potency Estimated in Mouse and Carcinogenic Potency Estimated in Rat for Several Chemicals.

a. B6C3F1 Mouse and Fischer 344 Rat.

b. B6C3F1 Mouse and Osborne Mendel Rat.

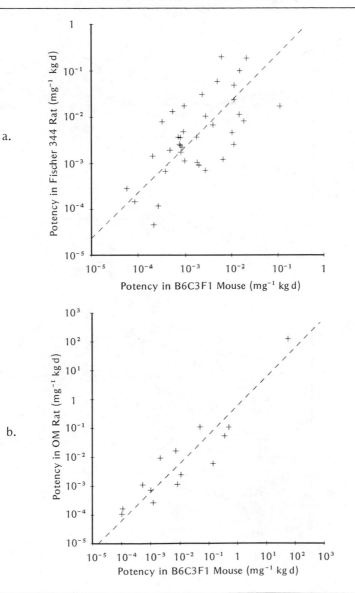

Source: Crouch (1981).

Figure 3-5. Relation Between Carcinogenic Potency Estimated in Animals and Carcinogenic Potency Estimated in Human Beings for Several Chemicals.

a. Rat and Man.

b. Mouse and Man.

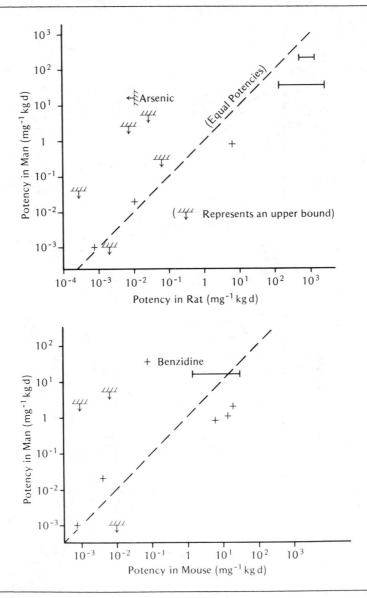

Source: Crouch and Wilson (1979).

PWR at any time, this experience can be used to obtain bounds on the probability per unit time (p) of such an accident occurring.

With the preceding assumption, which constitutes a model of such events, the best estimate of p is $1/400 = 2.5 \times 10^{-3}$ per reactor year, and p can be predicted to be less than 1.2×10^{-2} per year with 95 percent confidence; that is, if p is greater than 1.2×10^{-2}, there is less than 1 chance in 20 (5 percent) that 400 reactor years could have been accumulated with as few as one LOCA. Similarly a lower bound is obtained: 1.3×10^{-3} per year $< p$ with 95 percent confidence; that is, if p is less than 1.3×10^{-3} per year, there is less than 1 chance in 20 (5 percent) that 400 reactor years could have been accumulated with as many as one LOCA. We must stress that these numerical values are correct only if the assumptions (the model) are correct, and also that the probability per unit time of a LOCA does not directly give the probability per unit time of health hazards, because a LOCA does not necessarily lead to health hazards. Further analysis is necessary for evaluation of the health hazards.

Figure 3-6. Highly Simplified Example of Event Tree Leading to Serious Consequences for a Pressurized Water Reactor.

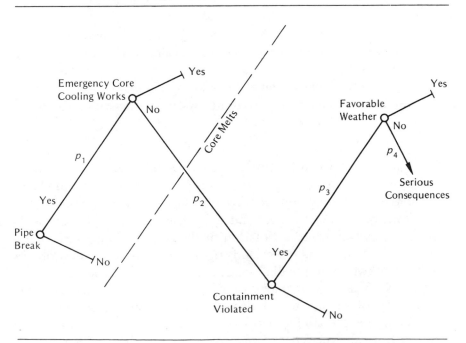

This form of analysis constitutes an all-at-once technique, but one that is less useful than the preceding example (chemical hazards) because it gives no clue as to how to reduce the risks. The limitation can be overcome if it is possible to analyze each event leading to risks as a sequence of well-understood events forming an event tree. A set of event trees would cover all possible cases leading to the final risky event.

The most well-known use of event tree analysis is, perhaps, the analysis of nuclear reactor accidents in the so-called Rasmussen report (Nuclear Regulatory Commission 1975). The procedure will be briefly outlined here with a highly simplified example from the report. The first step is identification of all possible sequences of events that may lead to serious consequences to public health and safety, followed by the separation of these sequences into segments that are approximately independent of each other. By analyzing each event in each sequence separately, using theory or past experience or both, the overall probability of occurrence of the whole sequence can be evaluated. Thus the most probable (highly simplified) sequence for catastrophic failure in a PWR is shown in Figure 3–6. The overall accident probability (with assumptions to be mentioned) is then equal to

> Probability of a pipe break (from theory and past data on other pipes)
>
> × probability of failure of emergency core cooling system (from a fault tree analysis)
>
> × probability of containment violation (more fault trees)
>
> × probability of unfavorable weather (past data on wind patterns, rainfall, and so on)
>
> $= p_1 \, p_2 \, p_3 \, p_4 \; .$

The accident described by this event tree is initiated by the break of a water pipe in the cooling system causing loss of coolant and resulting, if the emergency core cooling system subsequently fails, in the meltdown of the reactor core and the release of the fission products therein. This may cause a violation of the concrete containment vessel, so that if the wind direction is right the released fission products may be blown over population centers, possibly causing radiation overdoses to a large segment of the population. In each case the probability of the event and also its severity must be evaluated. As indicated, the probability (p_1) of a pipe break may be estimated from historical experience with pipes first in other industries, second in the limited experience of the nuclear industry, and finally with the theory of metal failure, while the likelihood (p_4) of unfavorable weather conditions together with an evaluation of how bad they may be can be obtained from weather records. The emergency core cooling system (ECCS) is designed to cool the reactor core in the event of loss of coolant, but there is a finite probability (p_2) that it will not work (for example, through failure of the equipment to switch on or through failure of the added emergency water to cool as planned). This probability is evaluated by using further trees called fault trees, the outcome of which is some failure mode for the ECCS. Similarly the probability (p_3) of failure of the containment is computed from known or calculable probabilities of prior events.

The basic assumptions of the event tree analysis technique can now be made clear.

1. The analysis is assumed complete, in the sense that the event trees calculated include all those that exist (or at least all those with a major contribution of risk) and lead to the final events analyzed, and also that the final events analyzed include all or the major portion of all possible events with adverse consequences.

2. The probabilities that are assumed to be independent of one another (p_1, p_2, p_3, p_4 in the event tree presented) are in fact independent. Any correlations known can be allowed for in the analysis; the danger comes from unknown correlation. The most obvious correlation can occur by deliberate sabotage of all systems simultaneously in the worst weather conditions.

The validity of the assumptions cannot be proved, and confidence in their validity for any particular study can be based only on the competence and thoroughness of the analysts and the robustness of the results under criticism from others. For reactor accidents, risks to public health arise only if there is a meltdown of a major part of the reactor core. Its position in the middle of the event tree helps us to eliminate as major contributors to risk those event trees where there is no meltdown. For most of the systems analyzed for risk by event tree analysis, it is unlikely that the overall results can be checked by experience except in the negative way of observing the lack of occurrence of large-consequence events, because one object of the analysis is to find those areas contributing most to the risk and improve them so as to lower the risk to the point where there would be little likelihood of the event occurring during the life of the system. Of course, the (higher probability) individual events on the event trees will be observed, so that the values used for their probability can be checked.

Event tree calculations have also been performed for the liquefied natural gas (LNG) industry (Science Applications, Inc., 1975; Simmons 1974; Keeney et al. 1978), the risk being a spill followed by fire or explosion. The principal event tree for large effects is (1) ship collision, (2) break of tank, (3) wind toward population center, (4) no ignition sources between the spill site and the population center (so that the LNG is not ignited before it reaches major population centers).

In the chemical industry, event trees are used in analyses of plant safety aimed at reducing hazards (Kletz 1978); they have been used (Health and Safety Executive 1978) in the estimation of risks from a particular industrial area containing oil refineries, LNG storage, liquefied petroleum gas (LPG) storage, liquid ammonia storage, and ammonium nitrate storage; and they are widely used in reliability analyses of many complex systems.

As a final class of risks and as an amusing example of the fact that zero risk is unattainable, consider certain risks that are predictable by very well verified physical theories but that involve events that have never been observed and probably never will be observed—events due to the inherent probablistic nature of certain phenomena. It may be recalled that the air we breathe is composed of molecules in constant motion, motion that is essentially random in nature. There is thus a finite but very small probability that all the air in a room could spontaneously move to one end of that room resulting in decompression of any occupant at the other end.

On an even more fundamental level, it appears that all matter obeys the laws of quantum mechanics, which are inherently probabilistic. As one consequence there is always a finite chance, albeit very small for macroscopic bodies, of any object spontaneously converting to a lower energy state even if there is a substantial energy barrier to be overcome. Because there apparently exist lower energy states for such bodies as the sun or earth, in the form of black holes, there is a theoretical possibility that the sun or earth might spontaneously convert to a black hole. Such an event has such a small probability that it is practically meaningless but nevertheless finite.

REFERENCES

Cairns, J. 1978. *Cancer—Science and Society.* San Francisco: W.H. Freeman and Company.

Crouch, E. 1981. "Uncertainties in Interspecies Extrapolations of Carcinogenicity," Presented at the International Symposium on the Health Effects of Tumor Promotion, Cincinnati, Ohio, October 12–15.

Health and Safety Executive. 1978. "Canvey: Investigation of Potential Hazards from Operations in the Canvey Island/Thurrock Areas." London: Her Majesty's Stationery Office.

Keeney, R.L.; R.B. Kulkani; and K. Nair. 1978. "Assessing the Risk of an LNG Terminal." *Technology Review* 81: 64.

Kletz, T. 1977. "Evaluate Risk in Plant Design." *Hydrocarbon Processing* 56: 297.

Meselson, M., and K. Russell. 1977. "Comparison of Carcinogenic and Mutagenic Potency." In *Origins of Human Cancer*, edited by H.H. Hiatt, J.D. Watson and J.A. Winsten, pp. 1473–1482. Cold Spring Harbor Laboratory.

Nuclear Regulatory Commission. 1975. "Reactor Safety Study: An Assessment of Accident Risks in U.S. Commercial Nuclear Power Plants." Wash–1400 (NUREG 75/014).

Science Applications, Inc. 1975. "LNG Terminal Risk Assessment Study for Los Angeles, California." Unpublished Report, December 22, Palo Alto.

Simmons, J.A. 1974. "Risk Assessment and Transport of LNG and LPG." Unpublished report for the Environmental Protection Agency, November 25, Washington, D.C.

U.S. Bureau of the Census. 1975. Historical Statistics of the United States, Colonial Times to 1970. Washington, D.C.

4 PERCEPTION OF RISK

Any politician would prefer a dead body to a frightened voter.

J. Dunster, U.K. Health and Safety Executive

The estimation of risk is moderately objective. Benefits are harder to analyze, vary from person to person, and depend upon the decision at issue. In particular cases benefits can be written down by the professional risk analyst, whose role may then be considered complete. The decision remains to be made, however, and in any given case the way in which risks and benefits are weighed depends upon how decision makers perceive risks or believe their constituencies perceive risks and how they decide which risks to accept.

Several approaches have been used to measure perceived risk. These may be categorized as the revealed preference method, the expressed preference method, and the implied preference method. The *revealed preference* method examines the historical behavior of society using statistical risk and benefit data. It presumes that society has adjusted automatically to an acceptable balance between risk and benefit. Starr (1969) was one of the original advocates of this approach. Several shortcomings of the revealed preference method can easily be seen. For example, it assumes that past relationships were desirable, whereas accepted levels of safety have depended on income distribution and social structures which may or may not now be considered desirable. Moreover, the method assumes that reason or choice would not have led to different preferences if the risks and benefits had been analyzed in advance and that risks and benefits can be accurately determined. Some of the measurement difficulties have been pointed out by Otway and Cohen (1975) and Fischhoff et al. (1980, 1977).

In order to determine the revealed preferences of society, one study (Baldewicz et al. 1974) determined baseline historical trends of risk levels for natural hazards such as floods, tornadoes, and lightning; man-made hazards such as commercial aviation, rail transportation, and rail grade crossings; and occupational hazards such as fire fighting, steel working, coal mining, and railroading. The study did not attempt to assess the benefits of the technologies associated with the hazards, however. Such studies and empirical data on risk levels, such as the National Safety Council's "Accident Facts," can be useful for comparison with public perception of risk levels determined by other methods.

Recent articles by Schwing (1980, 1979) and reviews by Cohen (1980) and Pollution Prevention (Crawley) Ltd. (1980) go further. For example, Cohen reviewed a number of decisions where money has been or is about to be spent to save lives. For each decision he estimates how much money society is willing to spend to save one life. His summary is reproduced here as Table 4–1. This set of numbers can be regarded as a historical evaluation of the constant γ in the formal risk benefit equation of Chapter 5. We notice a large variation but cannot tell whether it is due to intrinsic differences in society's valuation or due to the fact that in most cases a detailed risk benefit comparison was made only after the decision. This is certainly a list of what society has been willing to pay. An optimist could say it is what society will be willing to pay to reduce similar risks or even what society should be willing to pay. We do not go that far but, instead, put forward the tentative view that a well-executed assessment, well presented, will reduce the tendency for decision makers to pay much more or much less than the mean for risk reduction and, to this extent, to improve decision making. To do this the analyst must, inter alia, make clear the relations among public perception, myth, and objective reality. Whether or not this view is correct, we believe that a risk analyst does well to separate fact from opinion, indicating where assessment is based on fact and stating the assumptions in a form that makes clear where the judgment of the decision maker comes into play.

Table 4-1. Cost per Fatality Averted (1975 dollars) Implied by Various Societal Activities.

Item	Dollars per Fatality Averted
Medical Screening and Care	
Cervical cancer	25,000
Breast cancer	80,000
Lung cancer	70,000
Colorectal cancer:	
Fecal blood tests	10,000
Proctoscopy	30,000
Multiple screening	26,000
Hypertension control	75,000
Kidney dialysis	200,000
Mobile intensive care units	30,000
Traffic Safety	
Auto safety equipment—1966-70	130,000
Steering column improvement	100,000
Air bags (driver only)	320,000
Tire inspection	400,000
Rescue helicopters	65,000
Passive 3-point harness	250,000
Passive torso belt-knee bar	110,000
Driver education	90,000
Highway construc.—maint. practice	20,000
Regulatory and warning signs	34,000
Guardrail improvements	34,000
Skid resistance	42,000
Bridge rails and parapets	46,000
Wrong way entry avoidance	50,000
Impact absorbing roadside devices	108,000
Breakaway sign, lighting posts	116,000
Median barrier improvement	228,000
Clear roadside recovery area	284,000

(Table 4-1. continued overleaf)

Table 4-1. continued

Item	Dollars per Fatality Averted
Miscellaneous Non-radiation	
Expanded immunization in Indonesia	100
Food for overseas relief	5,300
Sulfur scrubbers in power plants	500,000
Smoke alarms in homes	250,000
Higher pay for risky jobs	260,000
Coal mine safety	22,000,000
Other mine safety	34,000,000
Coke fume standards	4,500,000
Air Force pilot safety	2,000,000
Civilian aircraft (France)	1,200,000
Radiation Related Activities	
Radium in drinking water	2,500,000
Medical X-ray equipment	3,600
ICRP recommendations	320,000
OMB guidelines	7,000,000
Radwaste practice—general	10,000,000
Radwaste practice—[131]I	100,000,000
Defense high level waste	200,000,000
Civilian high level waste	
No discounting	18,000,000
Discounting (1%/year)	1,000,000,000

Source: Cohen (1980).

In the *expressed preference* method, a sample of the public is asked directly to express preferences. Although the method accounts for current preferences, it is fraught with sampling difficulties. Not only is it difficult to obtain a large sample of individuals with the time and willingness to state their preferences, but the representativeness of any sample group can be challenged. Some individuals may be atypically uninformed; others may attempt to deliberately bias results. If carefully designed questions are used, however, these drawbacks may be less severe than those of the revealed preference method, which is retrospective in outlook.

The expressed preference method of evaluating risk perception has been used by Fischhoff et al. (1980, 1977) to assess the importance of various characteristics of risks and to rate subjects' perceptions of the total risks and benefits accruing to society from each of thirty activities and technologies. (Their work used as risk measure the total expected annual number of deaths in the United States.) The results showed that subjects believed that more beneficial activities could have higher levels of risk and that double standards of risk acceptance existed for certain characteristics of the risk, including voluntariness, controllability, familiarity, immediacy, and dread. The implication of the work is that any method for assessing the magnitude and acceptability of risks should consider all of these factors in concert, as well as benefits. Moreover, care must be exercised in defining terms such as *magnitude of perceived risks* and *acceptability of risks*, because these terms have different meanings to various individuals and might differ if different measures of risk are used. The relative rankings (see Figure 4-1) of hazards obtained using this method differ from those based strictly on objective measures (actual annual deaths in the United States). It appears that large risks are often underestimated and small ones overestimated.

In the third method for assessing public perceptions of risks, the *implied preference* approach, one examines the societal institutions that have been developed to cope with risk versus benefit trade-offs in the past. Legislative, judicial, and industrial standards reflect current balances achieved by society as a whole. Concepts such as reasonableness, best prevailing professional practice, and lowest practicable exposure, imply trade-offs among costs, risks, and benefits.

Of course, the existence of societal standards does not imply that future standards and factors influencing the public response will be the same as those of today. People's stated attitudes and their actual behavior often differ, people and governments may not be adequately informed, or they may desire unattainable risk levels. Moreover, different approaches to determining public preferences, including alternative formulations of questions, can elicit different responses. Thus, estimates of risk perception are not definitive and usually are representative of only a section of the population. Nevertheless, with a full appreciation of the difficulties of understanding and quantifying the public's perception of risks, this work should improve risk analysts' capability to assess and deal with future risks.

Figure 4-1. Relationship Between Judged Frequency and Actual Number of Fatalities per Year for 41 Causes of Death.[a]

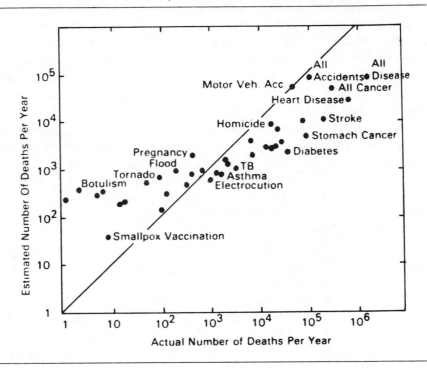

a. Respondents were informed of the actual number of motor behicle accidents.

Source: Lichtenstein et al. (1978).

FACTORS INFLUENCING RISK PERCEPTION

The literature on perception of risk and on methods for decision making about risk has been examined in several reviews and bibliographies (Clark and Van Horn 1976; Van Horn and Wilson 1976; Slovic et al. 1977, 1976; Fischhoff 1977; Fischhoff et al. 1980). The literature includes cognitive studies of human ability to judge and use probabilities (Slovic et al. 1974, Tversky and Kahneman 1976) and case studies of public protests over technological risks (Van Horn 1976, Ebbin and Kaspar 1974, Lawless 1974, Mazur 1975, Nelkin 1971).

Van Horn (1976) has indicated some of the diverse issues likely to arise when risks are considered. In general, public concern is aroused by risks in the following three categories:

1. Known, measured risks that have occurred in the past and might occur in the future
2. Risks of a potentially catastrophic nature, however small the probability
3. Risks that conflict with strongly held opinions on such matters as aesthetics, ecological values, or life-style benefits

Any of these can serve to arouse and sustain public attention. Once concern has been stimulated, a number of judgmental factors determine the response. Public attention may become focused on details that otherwise might seem to be trivial in comparison to other issues. If the risk analyst is prepared for such public attention, the analysis has a greater chance of being accepted. Following is a list of questions an analyst should consider generic to many societal risks, including those from nuclear power, liquefied natural gas, chemical carcinogens, and other technologies. The answers to the questions largely determine public's perception of risk.

1. What are the scientific and technological bases for estimating the expected risks and benefits?
   a. Is there general agreement over the basic facts among experts, or are there distinguished dissidents?
   b. Is there a good experimental basis for the facts?
   c. Is there a good theoretical basis for the facts?
   d. Has there been direct experience with the same or similar systems?
   e. Do the facts apply directly to the specific design or situation being assessed?
   f. Has the factual basis for the analysis been published?

If the answer to any of these questions is no, public suspicion can be intensified, but even a yes answer to all of them is no guarantee of public acceptance.

2. What is the probability of an accident with particular consequences?

   a. Would the worst accident be catastrophic? Has reliability of the probability of occurrence been determined? (To most people the magnitude is more important than the likelihood. In other words: It's not the odds; it's the stakes.)

   b. Is the risk well and simply described? Have the appropriate quantitative methods been used to determine the measures of risk?

   c. Are the risk estimates well defined? (Any uncertainty leads to anxiety about vulnerability, particularly for large consequence risks.)

   d. If a risk analysis assumes that safety precautions are necessary, will they be taken? Have all the important common mode failures (simultaneous failures traceable to a common initiating event) been considered in the risk analysis?

   e. Are the latent or delayed consequences small? Are they easily identifiable?

   f. Will the likelihood of an accident increase with time as equipment deteriorates or less well trained people enter the field? Does prior planning help to reduce the accident risk?

   g. Are there provisions for updating the accident data base and reevaluating the risks based on further experience?

   h. Will the risk calculation remain valid for a reasonably long time?

   i. Are there any circumstances under which the risk analysis would not apply? Have sabotage or deliberate acts been considered?

3. Can the risk be reduced and what will it cost?

   a. Does the risk level depend on physical safety precautions or solely on actions of (fallible) people? Which precautions are more fail-safe than others?

   b. Are the consequences reversible or irreversible? Could people cope with an accident or mitigate the results of an accident?

   c. Is there any experience or accepted prevailing practice for setting standards? Do the agencies and jurisdictions have adequate safety codes?

   d. Will the groups that accrue the benefits sustain the risks? Would reducing the benefits lessen the risks?

e. What groups are most likely to bear the consequences? Are the consequences similar for different groups?

f. Can affected groups be appropriately compensated for bearing an increased risk?

g. Are the same options open to persons who do not wish to enjoy the benefits or assume the risks?

Again, if the answer to a question is no, public concern can be aroused.

4. Is the risk acceptable? Is the distribution of risks and benefits fair?

a. Has a clear statement of both the benefits and risks been made?

b. Is the risk to each group worth the benefit gained? What are the specific risks and benefits to each group?

c. Is there a choice among alternatives? Were alternatives seriously considered? What are the risks and benefits of the alternatives? How do they compare to the original proposal? Apart from related alternatives might there be completely different ways to achieve similar benefits without these risks?

d. Do the affected groups have any control over the risk situation or over the design process?

e. Is the risk voluntarily assumed?

f. Is the risk visible? Is it continuous or intermittent? Will affected groups be aware of it?

g. Is the risk familiar to affected groups?

h. Is the consequence immediate or latent? How is the future to be "discounted," if at all? (Latent risks seem more acceptable because the benefits are enjoyed in the present. Smoking is a prime example.) Is discounting possibly large future risks (or benefits) a wise policy?

i. What are the project's future implications? Will other future options be foreclosed?

j. Are the potential risks and benefits comparable to similar risks and benefits present in today's society?

k. Is someone responsible in the event of an accident? Will available assets and insurance cover potential liabilities?

l. Have the media publicized the risks and benefits fairly?

    m. Is the decision process fair?

    n. Has the public been able to participate in an effective manner?

It should be emphasized that each case is different, but negative answers (or the lack of answers) to the questions listed can indicate the likely direction of public response. If answers to questions under (1) and (2) are not definitive, normative issues raised under (3) and (4) lead to increased public scrutiny and make acceptance less likely.

It is useful to go further and try to understand even more basic influences on risk perception. Ability to conceptualize and interpret risks is limited by various cognitive factors. Three examples have been demonstrated by Tversky and Kahneman (1974) that entail information being processed in a way that results in a persistent bias in interpretation.

The first cognitive factor is *representativeness.* Similarities between events are used to infer that one class of events, usually small in size, is representative of a large class of events. Often small samples may erroneously be viewed as reliable. Associated events may also be considered as representative of another class of events. As a hypothetical extreme case, a person might view a particular automobile as representative of the manufacturer's entire line or assume that limited data characterize the entire fleet. Such stereotyping may result in judgments that correspond to the stereotype rather than actual cases.

Anchoring, the second example, is a judgmental process by which a first approximation or estimate is progressively adjusted to account for subsequent occurrences. Where anchoring occurs, the adjustment is inaccurate. Thus, first estimates of a probability or of any numerical value seem to define a psychological range into which subsequent estimates will fall. Anchored estimates depend more heavily on the initial estimate than a statistical assessment of experience indicates, so that the phenomenon results in an inaccurate revision of probabilities. This occurs particularly for cases where the risk is delayed, like cigarette smoking, where individual initial adverse reactions are small, leading to perceptions of low risk.

Availability is a third cognitive factor resulting in misestimates of risk. It arises from the ease of recollection of events. One thinks, "If I can conceive of a number of ways for something to fail, the probability of failure must be high." The ease with which occurrences are brought to mind biases risk perception.

A number of other factors that can influence judgments of risk have been proposed in the literature. Some of these factors are implicitly addressed under question (4) listed earlier. One of the first to be suggested was that of the *voluntariness* of the risk. Starr (1972) suggested that risk acceptability depends on the extent to which we choose to be exposed to the risk situation; that is, we are loath to let others do to us what we happily do to ourselves. Lowrance (1976) and Fischhoff (1977) suggest that the following additional factors may contribute:

1. Immediacy of effect. Are the consequences immediate or delayed? Is there a latency period and how does it affect the perception of the risk situation? An action which has no consequences for 30 years is often put out of mind, although actions which might cause cancer after such a latency period appear to be exceptions to this generalization in some contexts, perhaps because of the horror with which cancer is regarded.

2. Availability of alternatives. Can alternatives be chosen to gain similar benefits with reduced risks? If the public can choose, the perception of the risk is often improved and acceptance may become easier.

3. Knowledge about risk. How well can risk analysts determine the risk? How large are the uncertainties? How well do persons exposed to the risks understand the risk, its probability, consequences, and uncertainties?

4. Necessity of exposure. How essential is exposure to the risky situation? If exposure is not essential, the acceptance is often less. But here again, one man's meat is another man's poison. We (the authors) do not dye our hair, but we do not believe it necessary to stop the use of (low-risk) hair dyes by others as long as those others are correctly informed of the risks.

5. Familiarity of risk. Old and familiar risks are accepted more readily than new and strange ones, particularly those (such as radiation) that cannot be seen.

6. Chronic versus catastrophic risk. Is the risk situation frequent or is it very rare with large numbers of fatalities possible?

7. Distribution of risk. Is the risk situation widespread? Does it affect average persons or especially sensitive persons?

8. Potential for misuse or abuse. If the technology is misused, do the risks increase significantly? How conceivable is misuse?

Tversky and Kahneman (1981) have emphasized the context dependence of judgments of risks. Just as many people will go to almost as much trouble to save $5 on a $15 outlay as $50 on a $150 outlay, so would some spend as much time and effort to reduce a risk from 10^{-7} deaths per year to 10^{-8} deaths per year as they would to reduce another risk from 10^{-3} deaths per year to 10^{-4} deaths per year. Yet if both risks applied to the whole population of the United States, the former corresponds to a reduction from 22 to 2 deaths per year, and the latter to reduction from 220,000 to 22,000 deaths per year. When these risks are expressed in terms of the numbers of deaths, it is clear that the smaller of the examples given should be ignored compared with the larger. Nevertheless, irrational concerns about reducing already small risks persist. This context dependence applies not only to different risks expressed in different ways, but even to identical risks so expressed. It appears, for example, that people are prepared to accept risks (that is, act in a risk-prone manner) when risks are posed as probabilities of loss of life, but are risk-averse if the same risks are posed as probabilities for saving lives.

We do not suggest that these considerations be explicitly introduced into the calculation of a risk, because that would also introduce an excessive degree of subjectivity on the part of the analyst. But the analyst must present results in a form useful to the decision maker who acts on behalf of the public, so that some consideration of these questions is essential.

As a general rule: If a risk analysis cannot be understood, it cannot be used. At all stages in presentation it is useful to compare the risk being calculated with other risks with which people may be more familiar from everyday life (see Chapter 7 for some common risks). Comparisons should not necessarily imply judgments. Cigarette smoke and air pollution both probably cause lung cancer, the former at least 20 times as much as the latter, yet cigarettes are smoked voluntarily and air pollution is involuntary, so even individuals who understand the numbers well can oppose air pollution while smoking like chimneys themselves.

As another example of comparison of common risks, we note that the Food and Drug Administration has under its jurisdiction many carcinogenic materials, among them the following: saccharin; aflatoxin B1, a toxin produced by mold growing on nut and corn products, present as a contaminant in milk, corn, and nuts; hair dyes, some of which contain the carcinogenic hair dye coupler 2-4 diaminoanisole (2-4 DAA) or lead acetate; vinyl chloride monomer (VCM), a carcinogen that migrates from some plastic bottles into food and drinks. Risks for each of them have been estimated from animal data, and the total number of cancers per year in all the United States have then been estimated—using the same methods in each case—as follows:

- Aflatoxin, 2,000 per year
- Saccharin, 500 per year
- 2-4 DAA, 1/2 per year
- VCM in bottles, 1/50 per year
- lead acetate, < 1/20 per year

Given such numbers, few would suggest that 100,000 times as much effort be expended on reducing the aflatoxin risk as on VCM in bottles, because no one knows how to do so except by banning milk and nuts; nonetheless this comparison should allow the setting of priorities for regulatory action.

Comparison can also be used to explain what a risk is. No one is born with an intuitive understanding for a risk of one in a million. It is an acquisition that can be made only by comparison. Pochin (1975) has discussed several risks and shows that an increase in annual risk of death of one in a million (10^{-6}) is accepted by most people. This increase is that obtained by smoking 1-1/2 cigarettes per year.

Another helpful comparison is to relate risk to loss of life expectancy. Life expectancy is a measure of the total risks facing people; small variations in the risks lead to corresponding variations in life expectancy. For fatal accidents, with an average loss of ~ 30 years of life per fatality, a risk of 1 in 10^6 gives a reduction of life expectancy of one-millionth of 30 years, or 16 minutes, so an annual accident risk of 1 in 10^6 reduces life expectancy by about 16 minutes per year of life. Since cancer occurs predominantly in higher age groups, cancer risks correspond to smaller loss of life expectancy, about 8 minutes for a cancer risk of 1 in 10^6. A convenient mnemonic is that smoking one cigarette takes 10 minutes, which is about the loss of life expectancy from smoking that same cigarette.

REFERENCES

Baldewicz, W.; G. Haddock; V. Lee; Prajoto; R. Whitley; and V. Denny. 1974. "Historical Perspectives on Risk for Large Scale Technological Systems." Unpublished report, UCLA-ENG-7485, University of California.

Clark, E.M., and A.J. Van Horn. 1976. "Risk Benefit Analysis and Public Policy: A Bibliography." Unpublished bibliography, Energy and Environmental Policy Center, Harvard University, November.

Cohen, B.L. 1980. "Society's Evaluation of Life Saving in Radiation Protection and Other Contexts." *Health Physics* 38 (January): 33.

Ebbin, S., and R. Kaspar. 1974. *Citizen Groups and the Nuclear Power Controversy: Uses of Scientific and Technological Information.* Cambridge, Massachusetts: MIT Press.

Fischhoff, B. 1977. "Cost Benefit Analysis and the Art of Motorcycle Maintenance." *Policy Sciences* 8: 177.

Fischhoff, B.; S. Lichtenstein; P. Slovic; R. Keeney; and S. Derby. 1980. "Approaches to Acceptable Risk, A Critical Guide." Unpublished report for the Nuclear Regulatory Commission, NUREG/CR-1614 (ORNL/Sub-76561/1). To be published by Cambridge University Press.

Fischhoff, B.; P. Slovic; S. Lichtenstein; S. Read; and B. Combs. 1977. "How Safe is Safe Enough?: A Psychometric Study of Attitudes Towards Technological Risks and Benefits." Unpublished report. Decision Research, Eugene, Oregon.

Lawless, E.W. 1974. "Technology and Social Shock—100 Cases of Public Concern Over Technology." Unpublished report, Midwest Research Institute for National Science Foundation/Research Applied to National Needs, Kansas City, Missouri.

Lichtenstein, S.; P. Slovic; B. Fischhoff; M. Layman; and B. Combs. 1978. "Judged Frequency of Lethal Events." *Journal of Experimental Psychology: Human Learning and Memory* 4: 551.

Lowrance, W. 1976. *Of Acceptable Risk: Science and the Determination of Safety.* Los Altos, California: William Kaufman, Inc.

Mazur, A. 1975. "Opposition to Technological Innovation." *Minerva* 13 (Spring): 58.

Nelkin, D. 1971. "Scientists in an Environmental Controversy." *Science Studies* 1: 145.

Otway, H.J. and J.J. Cohen. 1975. "Revealed Preferences: Comment on the Starr Benefit–Risk Relationships." Unpublished research memorandum, RM75–5, International Institute of Applied Systems Analysis, Laxenburg, Austria.

Pochin, E.E. 1975. "The Acceptance of Risk." *British Medical Bulletin* 31: 184.

Pollution Prevention (Crawley) Ltd. 1980. *Nuclear and Non–Nuclear Risk — an Exercise in Comparability.* Report EUR 6417 EN for the European Atomic Energy Community. Luxembourg: Office for Official Publications of the European Communities.

Schwing, R.C. 1980. "Trade-Offs." In *Societal Risk Assessment: How Safe is Safe Enough,* edited by R.C. Schwing and W.A. Albers, pp. 129–142. New York–London: Plenum Press.

_____. 1979. "Longevity Benefits and Costs of Reducing Various Risk." *Technological Forecasting and Social Change* 13: 333.

Slovic, P.; B. Fischhoff; and S. Lichtenstein. 1977. "Behavioral Decision Theory." In *Annual Review of Psychology* 28. Palo Alto, California: Annual Reviews, Inc.

_____. 1976. "Cognitive Processes and Societal Risk Taking." In *Cognition and Social Behavior,* edited by J.S. Carrol and J.S. Payne. Potomac, Maryland: L. Erlbaum Associates.

Slovic, P.; H. Kunreuther; and G.F. White. 1974. "Decision Processes, Rationality, and Adjustment to Natural Hazards." In *Natural Hazards, Local, National and Global,* edited by G.F. White. New York: Oxford University Press.

Starr, C. 1972. "Benefit–Cost Studies in Sociotechnical Systems." In *Perspectives in Risk Benefit Decision Making,* Committee on Public Engineering Policy, National Academy of Engineering, Washington, D.C.

_____. 1969. "Social Benefit versus Technological Risk: What Is Our Society Willing to Pay for Safety?" *Science* 165: 1232.

Tversky, A., and D. Kahneman. 1981. "The Framing of Decisions and the Psychology of Choice." *Science* 211: 453.

_____. 1974. "Judgment under Uncertainty: Heuristics and Biases." *Science* 185: 1124.

Van Horn, A.J. 1976. "Public Concerns over the Siting and Safety of Liquified Natural Gas Facilities." Unpublished report, Energy and Environmental Policy Center, Harvard University, November.

Van Horn, A.J., and R. Wilson. 1976. "The Status of Risk Benefit Analysis." Unpublished report, BNL–22282, Brookhaven National Laboratory, December.

5 COMPARISON OF RISK AND BENEFIT

That's how I judge pain, Lucille. . . . Will it hurt more than a punch in the nose or less than a punch in the nose?

From a Charles Schulz' Peanuts cartoon.

What is the object of evaluating risks? The many reasons include academic interest, the desire to analyze risks in order to find ways of reducing them, and the need for input for decisions about taking various actions. It is the last reason that is of concern in this chapter, which treats the question: Are the risks of the action big enough to outweigh any of its benefits? The answer may be used as one input in a decision process.

In many cases the decision is taken very simply. The risk may be so large that once it is perceived something is done about it almost independent of cost, as in the case of evacuation of the populace around spilled toxic chemicals. In other cases the risk may be obviously so small that it is not worth the trouble to think about it; an example is occupational risk to a waitress sweeping up spilled saccharin powder.

These cases—the very large risk and the very small—are barely worth calling decisions, because they involve no controversy. Still other risks may belong to either one or the other of these two categories but are not so perceived either because the calculation has not been done or because the calculation is complex enough or the risk is badly enough perceived that it is not understood when it is done (occasional hair dye use is not very dangerous; the smoking habit is).

Up to the present, risk analysis has mainly been used to take risks in the third category (unknown) and put them into the first (large) or second category (negligible). For this purpose a great deal of precision in the calculation is not necessary; in the first case (large risk) it is obvious that the risk exceeds the benefit and in the second case (negligible risk) it is obvious that the benefit exceeds the risk. For these cases little more need be written, but a procedure exists for assessing and aiding decisions in more marginal cases.

Various criteria have been advanced as appropriate for explicit consideration of risks. These include the following:

- *Zero risk.* On this criterion any action that involves any risk at all should be rejected. The definiteness and simplicity of decision processes based on such a criterion are soon seen to be false, however, because, although the criterion may be stated, it is not possible to carry it out. Every action, including inaction, has some risk associated with it, either directly or through indirect risks; for example, to build thicker and thicker walls as protection leads statistically to deaths and injuries in cement production and in the building trade.

- *As low as reasonably achievable* (ALARA). All risks should be made as low as reasonably achievable in any action dependent on the decision process, according to this criterion. A decision rule is needed for specifying what is reasonable, a rule that ultimately depends on physical limits (say, how thick a roof can be constructed) and the cost of implementation (how much more it will cost to brace the walls in order to support the thicker roof). Such decision rules may be made ad hoc, case by case, or may specify arbitrary cost figures. Although workable, they lead to inconsistencies in effective valuation of various risks and are inefficient in the sense that a more consistent criterion would be capable of saving more lives at the same cost or the same number at lower cost.

- *Best available control technology* (BACT). The problem with trying to reduce risks using the best available technology is in knowing what is the best available technology. Usually availability is taken to mean commercial availability, in a tested design and at a cost that is not exorbitant. In the case of removal of sulfur oxides from power plant exhaust gases, it is possible to build equipment that would be more effective than that currently considered the best available control technology, but the running costs would be impractically high, so such equipment has not been built on a large scale and is unlikely to be built. This was the criterion adopted by the U.S. Congress for the clean air acts of the 1970s.

- *Risk/cost/benefit analysis.* This criterion requires that explicit account be taken of values to be assigned to various risks, so that they may be traded against the costs and benefits. It should be noted that the other three criteria all implicitly assign a value to the risks they are designed to control but do so inconsistently.

Because all the foregoing criteria implicitly or explicitly imply a set of values for risks, cost, and benefits, we advocate the use of explicit risk/cost/benefit analysis, in which the values assigned are explicitly recognized and discussed. The actual analysis performed will depend on the particular case, but we can distinguish two important generic types. The first is *analysis of a single action*, in which a decision is required on whether to go ahead, based on the expected overall costs, risks, and benefits expected. The second, which allows considerable simplification, is the *comparison of different actions* that have identical or very similar benefits or costs or risks. In both cases a set of common problems may occur, which has led to argument over the use of this type of analysis.

The first problem the analyst meets in using this method concerns the time lapse between action and risk, cost, or benefit. The risks of any action may not all accrue at one time. Accidents usually occur at the time of the action, but cancer and disease caused by air pollution, for example, can occur many years later. Moreover, there are even later effects of environmental pollution. Toxic chemical wastes or radioactive substances can enter the biosphere hundreds of years or more after the actions causing them. The risk of mortality therefore is not a simple quantity but a function of time, $R(t)$ say, and similarly the other measures of risk vary with time. Benefits do not all occur at once either. The risks of coal mining start when the coal is mined; but the benefits come much later, when it is burned. There is a stream of benefits $B(t)$ and of costs $C(t)$.

Risks and benefits are usually incommensurate quantities, although of course monetary costs and benefits are both measured in monetary units such as dollars. For decision making it is usual to try to put them on a common basis by, for example, estimating society's willingness to pay to reduce a risk or to forgo a benefit. In order to do this, one may introduce factors $\alpha(B, t)$, $\beta(C, t)$, and $\gamma(R, t)$, which, at some time t reduce, respectively, benefits, costs, and risks to a common scale, so that, on this scale, the part of net worth of the action attributable to time t is

$$\alpha(B, t)\, B(t) - \beta(C, t)\, C(t) - \gamma(R, t)\, R(t) \ .$$

(We are considering benefits positive and subtracting costs and risks.) To solve the problem of adding such valuations at different times t in order to obtain the total effect, we introduce a time factor $D(t)$, which discounts the value at time t to time zero (at the moment the decision is made) and hence obtain a net present value (NPV) of

$$\text{NPV} = \sum_{t=0}^{T} D(t)\, \left\{ \alpha(B, t)\, B(t) - \beta(C, t)\, C(t) - \gamma(R, t)\, R(t) \right\} \ .$$

T is the time horizon for the analysis, the distance into the future that will be taken into account in making any decision. In business decisions using similar methodology, T is usually small (one to ten years), but for a full cost-risk-benefit analysis it may be very large. The usual choice for a discounting function $D(t)$ is the standard economist's choice:

$$D(t) = \frac{1}{(1 + r)^t} \ ,$$

where r is a discount rate. This has the merit of simplicity and of consistency; using this choice and only this choice, one would still make the same decision at any arbitrary future time, and the decision will still appear correct at any time after it is made, provided the results are evaluated using the same discount rate. The simple prescription for decisions is that the action should proceed if NPV is positive and should not proceed if NPV is negative.

The application of a discount factor $D(t)$, especially the same discount factor, to all of benefits, costs, and risks may be questioned, especially for risks. It is equivalent to saying, for example, that the discounted amount the risk takers are willing to pay in the present to save a life in the future decreases as the time of that life-saving gets more remote. This is not unreasonable, however, if the amount discounted is an accurate reflection of the cost of saving that life, since economic use of the discounted amount from now until the future data will yield a return sufficient to bear the cost of saving the life. Raiffa, Schwartz, and Weinstein (1977) argue that lives should be discounted at the same rate as money for this reason. Indeed few people worry about their great grandchildren living 50 years hence, an attitude which corresponds to discounting these descendants' lives at a rate greater than ~8 percent. If the amount used is an estimate of the value of a life (determined subjectively, for example), this argument may break down, but this can be taken care of in our formalism, as we will show. The present furor over nuclear and other toxic waste disposal suggests a trend toward low discount rates for future risks. It has been suggested (Cochran 1979; Egan 1978; Martin and Egan 1979) that no subsequent generation should be exposed to a risk greater than that to which we are willing to expose ourselves $(D(t) = 1)$. It is unclear whether this is a permanent public opinion or a temporary fad.

The second major problem to take into account is the evaluation of factors α, β, γ that reduce benefits, costs, and risks to common units. For benefits and costs that are easily stated in monetary terms, the factors may be taken as unity (we assume monetary common units). Much criticism of risk/benefit analysis can be traced to discussions about the validity of using such numbers, and even where the basic validity is not questioned the actual value that should be taken is questioned. In most cases, it is the evaluation of γ that excites most passion, so we will discuss γ, but similar comments apply to nonmonetary costs and benefits. There is an extensive literature on this problem (Cohen 1980; Schwing 1979; Linnerooth 1975; Schelling 1968; Zeckhauser 1975; Zeckhauser and Shepard 1976; Thaler and Rosen 1973).

The use of a form γR for the monetary cost of a risk R is an approximation to the use of the economist's idealized utility function. We are attempting to obtain a measure of the utility of a risk, measured by some risk measure with value R, by assigning a value γ per unit of risk. We note the following points, often misunderstood by detractors of this approach:

The coefficient γ need not be a constant, independent of the size of the risk. For example, for individuals the value of γ may increase or decrease as R increases, depending on the circumstances, so $\gamma = \gamma(R)$; it is a function of the risk. Such behavior is perfectly consistent, may be theoretically derived from certain utility models

(Howard 1980), and is easy to understand heuristically. Consider an individual faced with a risk of death of negligibly small value, say 10^{-9} probability of dying. That person would probably be prepared to pay a very small amount in order to avoid such a risk. Similarly, for a larger, but still small risk, say 10^{-6} probability of dying, the person would pay a larger amount, possibly 10^3 times as much, in exchange for avoidance. If the risk presented gets large enough, however, the limit of the ability of the individual to pay may be reached, so that the amount per unit of risk (γ) must thereafter decrease (Figure 5–1). An individual who makes decisions on this basis is displaying risk-prone behavior.

Different behavior may occur if an individual is invited to take a certain risk in exchange for money. For small enough risks the amount of money required in exchange for taking the risk may be proportional to the size of the risk, but for large enough risks (approaching certainty of death) it is plausible that no amount of money would provide sufficient inducement (Figure 5–2). This leads to a value of γ that increases as R increases. An individual who makes decisions on such a basis is displaying risk-averse behavior.

The two different behaviors for γ could be exhibited by the same individual, depending on the circumstances. It is thus quite possible for γ to take on different values depending upon the way in which the risk occurs. Some attempts to discover how society actually behaves under various circumstances have been made by Griesmeyer, Simpson and Okrent (1979), and by Litai (1980). (See also the subsequent discussion of distributional equity.)

In addition to variations with the size and nature of the risk, γ may also depend on time t, so $\gamma = \gamma(R, t)$. If what is to be measured is the actual cost of repairing the damage caused when the risk is realized (if this is possible), then the argument about discounting is valid, so that, in this case, γ may be taken independent of time insofar as the actual costs are independent of time (we are speaking of the economist's "real" costs here). However, if it is necessary to use an individual's valuation of his or her life (for example), this may not be true, for such a valuation may vary with time. The simplest such case is if the valuation varies at the same rate as the (real) interest (discount) rate; for example, a valuation that regards a life as being worth a fixed fraction of the total economic activity rather than the fixed amount of economic activity implied by the real cost case. Then the applied discount rate in the NPV equation and the increas-

Figure 5-1. Amount Paid per Unit of Risk (γ) to Avoid a Risk.

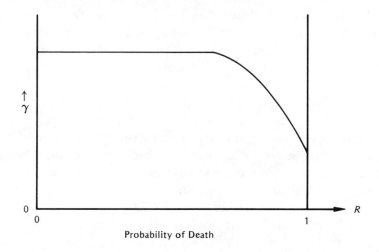

Probability of Death

Figure 5-2. Amount Required per Unit of Risk (γ) to Take a Risk.

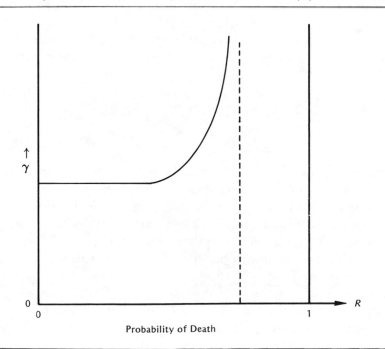

Probability of Death

ing value of γ exactly cancel, so that the present valuation of a life is identical for lives at any time in the future—or alternatively, so that in the future greater absolute value is assigned to a life.

The third major problem to be considered is that of distributional inequity: The costs, risks, and benefits do not necessarily accrue to the same individuals or populations. Thus the benefits derived from electricity production are shared among a population extending many miles from a coal-fired power station, but the amenity costs (loss of visual amenity, excess traffic for fuel transport, higher pollution) are largely borne by the neighbors of the station. Although it is usual to compensate the neighbors to some extent through reduced property taxes, since the power station usually pays substantial property taxes that subsidize the local neighborhood, there nevertheless remains inequity in distribution of the benefits, costs, and risks.

It must be recognized that distributional inequity may arise from any decision however—it is not unique to decisions suggested by risk/cost/benefit analysis—and exists because of the imperfections of compensation mechanisms. If the choices discussed thus far are correctly made, the net present value obtained will be correct for the whole population (and will take into account individuals at high risk, for example) and the formalism may be used to find values of the NPV for subpopulations. Thus for each risk, cost, benefit of type i and individual j to be included, the NPV should be evaluated as follows:

$$
\mathrm{NPV} = \sum_{t=0}^{T} \sum_{j} \sum_{i} D_j(t) \left\{ \alpha_j(B_{ij}, t) B_{ij}(t) - \beta_j(C_{ij}, t) C_{ij}(t) \right.
$$
$$
\left. - \gamma_j(R_{ij}, t) R_{ij}(t) \right\} \quad .
$$

By restricting the summations over the population (index j) one can obtain the NPV for subpopulations. Theoretically, but not practically, this would allow the design of compensating mechanisms that could ensure that every individual benefited (if the NPV is positive). In practice, this is the field of political compromises—adjusting the actions so that some groups benefit while others suffer a loss that is not too large. With proper choice of α, β, γ, the effect of placing large burdens of cost or risk on individuals or small groups should already be accounted for in the NPV sum, because in most such cases the required value of γ (for example) will be that obtained when offering money in exchange for taking a risk and will thus probably increase rapidly for large values of risk.

Although the basic NPV equation may be useful for understanding details of the analysis, it is not usually useful for its presentation. Large approximations are usually made in the estimation of the benefits, the risks, and the costs. Similar approximations may be made in estimating the coefficients α, β, γ, without altering the outcomes. For example, if the cost or risk terms are included without discounting (or equivalently by making the terms β, γ increase with time at the discount rate), and the NPV is still positive, it is clear that the benefits outweigh risks and costs. If all the risks are small (the risk to all individuals is small enough), a constant value of γ is probably appropriate (independent of the size of the risk). This is probably true for all probabilities of death below about 10^{-6} to 10^{-7} per year, as may be judged by consulting the tables of actual risks affecting individuals in the United States shown in Chapter 7.

If it is required to evaluate which is the better of two options providing similar benefits, rather than making decisions about a single scheme, some simplifications may be made. The simplest case is that in which both benefits and costs are identical but the risks differ, in which case all that is required is the evaluation of the difference.

$$
\mathrm{NPV}^{(1)} - \mathrm{NPV}^{(2)} = \sum_{t=0}^{T} \left\{ \sum_i \sum_j D_j(t)\, \gamma_j\, (R_{ij}^{(1)}, t)\, R_{ij}^{(1)}(t) - \right.
$$

$$
\left. - \sum_l \sum_m D_m(t)\, \gamma_m\, (R_{lm}^{(2)}, t)\, R_{lm}^{(2)}(t) \right\} \quad ,
$$

where (1) and (2) refer to the two options. Because all that is being evaluated are the effects of risks, the absolute values of the coefficients γ do not affect the sign of the comparison but only the relative value. In this case only the relative values of different risk measures are required, while problems of discounting of the risks and distributional inequity remain, as represented by sums over possibly different risk types (i and l), possibly different populations (j and m), and the discount factor $D(t)$.

Although even this looks a formidable task, practical cases suggest that it is possible to manage with fairly simple approximations. For example, in the examination of the option of using X rays for screening whole populations or subgroups of populations for potentially fatal diseases, almost the only risk of concerns is that of death or disability either from the disease or from a cancer induced by the X rays. The benefit is the possibly early detection and cure of the disease. Because benefit and risks are both in the same units (probabilities of dying or disability), there is no problem of intercomparison. To extend the analysis would require the introduction of the cost of the screening (assuming one finds that the risks are decreased by such screening). Even though an absolute evaluation of the value of such a screening program then requires a valuation of the risks, this problem may be avoided if only comparisons between different screening options are required, for then the cost effectiveness may be a suitable comparison measure.

In the ultimate analysis, the values of α, β, and γ depend upon individual perception of risk. They differ for different individuals and for different types of risk (as we suggested by use of subscripts), although we suggest that in many analyses representative values are sufficient for public policy purposes.

REFERENCES

Cochran, T. 1979. "Proceedings of Conference on High Level Radioactive Waste Forms." U.S. Nuclear Regulatory Commission NUREG/CP 0005. Denver, Colorado.

Cohen, B.L. 1980. "Society's Evaluation of Life Saving in Radiation Protection and Other Contexts." *Health Physics* 38 (January): 33.

Egan, D.J. 1978. "Risk Assessment in Support of Environmental Standards, EPA's High Level Radioactive Waste Standards." Paper presented at the American Institute of Chemical Engineering, November.

Griesmeyer, J.M.; Simpson; and D. Okrent. 1979. "The Use of Risk Aversion in Risk Acceptance Criteria." Unpublished report UCLA–ENG–7970, Department of Engineering, University of California.

Howard, R.A. 1980. "On Making Life and Death Decisions." In *Societal Risk Assessment: How Safe is Safe Enough?*, edited by R.C. Schwing and W.A. Albers, pp, 89–106. New York–London: Plenum Press.

Linerooth, J. 1975. "The Evaluation of Life Saving — A Survey." Unpublished report IIASA RR–75–21. Laxenburg, Austria: International Institute of Applied Systems Analysis.

Litai, D. 1980. "A Risk Comparison Methodology for the Assessment of Acceptable Risk." Ph.D. dissertation, Massachusetts Institute of Technology.

Martin, J.S., and D.J. Evans. 1979. Testimony to the Committee on Interior and Insular Affairs, U.S. House of Representatives, January 25.

Raiffa, H.; W. Schwartz; and M. Weinstein. 1977. "Evaluating Health Effects of Societal Decisions and Programs." In *Decision Making in the Environmental Protection Agency*, vol. 2B. National Academy of Sciences.

Schelling, T. 1968. In *Problems in Public Expenditure*, edited by S.B. Chase. Washington, D.C.: The Brookings Institution.

Schwing, R.C. 1979. "Longevity Benefits and Costs of Reducing Various Risks." *Technological Forecasting and Social Change* 13: 333–345.

Thaler, S. and S. Rosen. 1975. "The Value of Saving a Life." In *Household Production and Consumption*, National Bureau of Economic Research, New York.

Zeckhauser, R. 1975. "Procedures for Valuing Lives." *Public Policy* 23: 419.

Zeckhauser, R. and D. Shepard. 1976. "Where Now For Saving Lives." *Law and Contemporary Problems* 40, No. 5.

6 A PRESCRIPTION FOR USEFUL ANALYSIS
Case Studies

The consideration of [the] risk-benefit ratio is basic to any intelligent discussion of any problem involving technology and society, and is all too often ignored in the utterances of consumer advocates and industry spokesmen.

> Jean Meyer. 1976. In the foreward to *Eaters Digest*, by M.F. Jacobson. New York: Doubleday (Anchor Books).

In previous chapters we discussed the status of risk analysis, the way in which the public perceive risks, and the extent to which risks are accepted. We also discussed criticisms that have been leveled at the concept of risk analyses and explained our view that these criticisms should be leveled only at inadequate or incorrect risk analyses and not at the concept in general. The present chapter supplements the previous ones by a prescription we believe can be usefully followed and by critical discussions of some selected cases in which risk analysis has been used in the past. These critiques will show, in a way no general theoretical discussion can, the strengths and weaknesses of the method.

The nine cases we shall present are some examples of risk analysis we have been able to discover in contemporary American society. It is not encouraging that formal calculation of risks has been so rarely used and described; it is less encouraging still that when these nine cases are examined in detail major flaws and weaknesses can be discovered. We are heartened, however, by the realization that many of the flaws can easily be remedied and that in at least one case (saccharin) common sense filled in the gaps.

Before beginning a detailed discussion of individual studies, it is useful to picture an idealized scheme (Figure 6-1) of the complete decision process, and the place of risk assessment within it. Information is passed from scientist, engineer, and economist to risk assessor and to cost and benefit assessors. The results of these assessments and comparisons between them are made available to the decision-

Figure 6-1. Idealised Scheme for Risk Analysis.

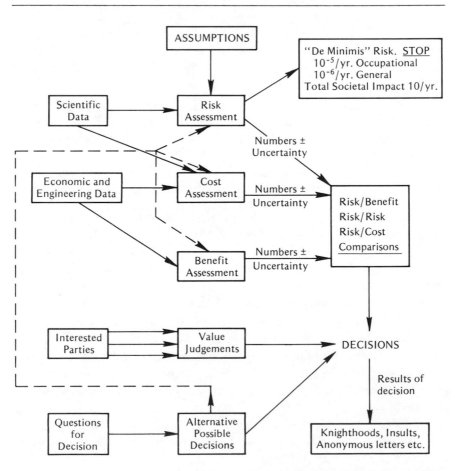

maker who might be bureaucrat, politician, or any ordinary citizen, depending on the analysis being performed. Value judgments from interested parties such as the public, unions, churches, and industry are also available to the decisionmaker, whose decision might be swayed by such judgments. However, the initial assessments should be performed independently of such value judgments; the scientist, economist, and engineer should be distinct from the assessors, and all should be distinct from the decisionmaker, even though the same person may play different roles at different times. The assessors have to know what are the questions for decision and have some idea of the alternatives open in order to provide comprehensive and illuminating assessments. These inputs to the assessment process are indicated by dotted lines on Figure 6-1, since they provide the framework for the assessments rather than the quantitative data for their completion.

There is an analogy between the process shown in Figure 6-1 and the Anglo-Saxon legal system which indicates some of the strengths and weaknesses to be expected. A judge decides on questions of law while the jury—the assessors—decide questions of fact after being instructed on what is legally relevant. A historical example from the United Kingdom shows how this separation of function may be upset. In Cromwell's time a law was passed making it illegal to kiss in public. The law may have been sensible but the penalty was death. All juries considered this draconian, and so violated the rules separating the legal framework and the assessment of fact, with the result that no person accused of the crime was convicted. Similarly, a group of assessors asked an inappropriate question or suspicious that their assessment might be used in a foolish manner, might well provide a biased assessment.

The last part of Figure 6-1 represents a short cut to be used when risks are very small. If the risk assessment shows a 'de minimis' risk (from the legal maxim 'de minimis non curat lex' or 'the law is not concerned with trifles'), the rest of the procedure of risk analysis should be unnecessary. The numbers suggested for such a 'de minimis' risk are: occupational risk of death—1 in 100,000 (10^{-5}) per year; individual general public risk of death—1 in 1,000,000 (10^{-6}) per year; total societal impact—10 deaths per year. Only risks larger than these, which are suggested by comparison with current values of risks given in Chapter 7, need be given further detailed attention. The actual numbers 10^{-5}, 10^{-6}, and 10 should not be regarded as sacrosanct and the perception of different risks should be taken into account in choosing to regard any given risk as negligible, but they indicate the correct order of magnitude.

The most objective part of the problems is often the calculation of risk, and this is the part that has usually been attempted. Even here, the analyses have been inadequate. The assumptions may be too restrictive or simplistic, the data base sparse, inadequate, or unreliable, the analytic method too complex, inconsistent, or merely untested. All too often these flaws arise from the fact that the time allowed for analysis is too short or the funds too small, although even the more lavishly funded analyses can have their shortcomings.

The weaknesses of risk analysis should not cause despair even among those who seek an ideal world. When risk analysis is properly viewed as an aid to decisionmaking rather than as the decision making process itself, even an incomplete analysis can be useful so long as the incompleteness is admitted. Any good and useful analysis has, therefore, a clear summary of assumptions and a clear statement of uncertainties. All too often a risk analysis report has 400 pages of detailed calculation with only one sentence describing important omissions—a sentence such as "We have not considered sabotage of the facilities." Worse still, this sentence either is lost in the middle of the long report or is part of a badly worded and obscure recommendation.

Our prescription for a good analysis is to avoid such problems as far as possible. A good risk/benefit analyst can calculate the tractable parts of the problem or put bounds on the risk and identify the intangible factors. The user of the analysis can focus on the intangible factors that are the most important and significant factors in the decision. Without the risk/benefit analysis as a guide the decision maker has no suggestion that anyone has thought the problem through in all its detail.

A PRESCRIPTION FOR USEFUL ANALYSIS

The most important aspect of a risk analysis, in our view, is simplicity of exposition. Contrary to the naive view of some critics this need not mean any loss of precision. Careful use of language and precision of statement is very important to convey understanding.

Simplicity of exposition may, on occasion, require that the risk be presented more pessimistically (conservatively) than is the considered view of the risk analyst or the majority of his or her scientific peers. This need not mean definitive acceptance of a pessimistic position, although in many cases simplicity and ease of understanding enable a decision to be made with speed and firmness, which in itself can have advantages compared with the problems created by an excess of caution.

With these general observations we proceed to the detail of our recommended procedures, categorizing the principal steps in a risk/benefit analysis as follows:

1. Defining objectives and goals
2. Identifying assumptions
3. Identifying and measuring risks and costs
4. Identifying and measuring benefits
5. Specifying and highlighting uncertainty
6. Aggregating and comparing risks, costs, and benefits
7. Identifying groups at risk and recipients of benefits
8. Addressing inequities in the distribution of risks, costs, and benefits
9. Developing decision criteria that include any applicable constraints
10. Communicating and summarizing results

Before proceeding to the illustration of these steps in practice in our nine selected cases, let us comment on each step.

Defining Objectives and Goals

The first step is to ascertain what decision is to be considered. Should saccharin be banned, for example? Once the range of possible decisions is understood, the analyst can decide what facts have to be assembled to help make the decision.

As the aim of risk analysis should be to improve decisions and not to substitute for them, analyses that identify the prospective decision maker and are aimed at answering specific questions are most likely to be useful and therefore successful. Illustrated in Chapter 2 were difficulties that arise when the questions asked are not specific enough. There is no harm in covering many possibilities (see the next step) in a format that allows the answering of many questions, but it is important that specific questions be formulated.

Moreover, decisions on risks should be made in such a way that new scientific data can be accommodated and that appropriate incentives are present to acquire new data. A rigid standard can stifle the acquisition of new data because if offers no financial or other advantage to anyone to acquire data.

The accumulation of sufficient data may be incorporated as one objective of a risk/benefit analysis. If, as is often the case, the empirical data are an inadequate basis for precise calculation of a risk, a reasonably conservative (and inevitably less accurate) estimate can be made. Then the person or organization that would gain from a more accurate evaluation of the risk has an incentive to acquire additional data.

Identifying Assumptions and Alternatives for Comparison

Step 2 would, for the example of air pollution, state the assumption that the death rate is proportional to air pollutant concentration at low levels or the alternative assumption that there is a definite threshold below which there is no effect.

A review of the best available scientific evidence for the assumptions is essential. In general, the risk analysis should be based on firm data from observation or experiment. But the use of the word *assumption* implies that firm data are lacking or ambiguous and that the assumptions are based on theory rather than fact.

The review must therefore include a discussion of all shades of opinion so that decision makers, who will thereby have the opposing views brought to their attention, can have the best possible guidance. The list of assumptions is so important that it may need to be repeated at several places in the analyst's report. Analyses of all alternatives may be too lengthy; instead it may be more useful to do analyses only on those alternatives that, although agreeing with available data, provide bounds on the results.

Identifying and Measuring Risks and Costs

It is worth emphasizing that the stated quantification of risks and costs should be only to the level of accuracy necessitated by the problem. Very often risks are not known to better than a factor of 3; in such cases, specification of the risk to three significant figures implies a greater degree of knowledge than is warranted and obscures understanding. Likewise, when the risk is very small, the precision needed is not great, for where the calculated risk is small it is most probable that some intangible risks and costs that are being omitted are larger than the calculated ones. This possibility must be clearly stated—preferably repeatedly. It is vital to itemize the risks that are specifically included and attempt to list everything (of plausible or possible importance) that is specifically excluded.

Identifying and Measuring Benefits

The nature of the decision being considered is always crucial (see Chapter 2). In a decision of the U.S. Occupational Safety and Health Administration (OSHA) involving employees, for example, there are always at least three distinct types of benefit as a result of accepting a risk: a benefit to society as a whole, a benefit to a manufacturer from increased profits, and a benefit to the employee from a job that pays an attractive wage or salary. If there is no benefit in any one of these categories the proposed action is unlikely to take place. In another case the groups who benefit may be different, but the benefits must be calculated for each group.

Specifying and Highlighting Uncertainty

Criticisms of the claimed accuracy of risk/benefit analyses often have merit. Systematic biases, such as the tendency to overestimate costs of compliance with a regulation by underestimating human ingenuity, must be acknowledged; similarly, future benefits of a new technology can easily be ignored. More important, however, is a tendency to ignore future risks. For example, even now the cost of possible failure of proposed dams is not explicitly considered in deciding whether to proceed with their construction.

Every number should have an error estimate attached to it, computed in as rigorous a way as the initial number. Only rarely is the error zero (bounds might have zero error in one direction but not in the other). The error estimate shows just how bad the statistics really are, to overcome the observed tendency of most people to overestimate the significance of small samples.

The Aggregation and Comparison of Risks, Costs, and Benefits

It is in the comparison of risks with benefits, as was shown in the last chapter, that most philosophical attacks are made upon risk/benefit analysis. Careful exposition is required to minimize opportunities for misunderstanding. The problem arises because it is necessary to compare incommensurate quantities, perhaps a risk to life on one hand and a monetary profit to society on the other.

We recommend avoiding unnecessary philosophical discussion and concentrating on the issue at hand instead. In deciding, for example, whether to spend money for major surgery or for prevention of cancer or for basic research, one issue is the best allocation of limited resources—a cost effectiveness problem. Often, publicity hounds emphasize the dramatic by discussing the value of a human life, an imponderable question irrelevant to the decision at issue. Because of the tendency to overdramatize this aspect of risk/benefit comparison, both the risks and benefits, with their incommensurate nature emphasized, must be clearly brought through to the end of the discussion.

Identifying the Groups at Risk and the Groups Who Benefit—Disaggregation of the Risk/Benefit Equation

Often it is easier to calculate an average risk to people in society than to calculate the risk to an individual or small groups. The average does not necessarily give a realistic representation of the real world, and the disaggregation may be essential to any decision. The analyst may decide to calculate separately for society as a whole, for subgroups, and finally for individuals. For example, the overall loss of life from coal mining in the United States is about 1,000 lives per year, including deaths from black lung disease. This is not a large number compared with total annual deaths, but in proportion to the number of coal miners it is large. Society has the benefit of coal; miners have only their wage.

Historically the average risk to society has been considered most important. Thus Frances Hutcheson wrote "That action is best which requires the greatest happiness for the greatest number" (Treatise II "Concerning Moral Good and Evil"), and John Dryden commented "Better one suffer than a nation grieve" (Absalom and Achitophel). However, this view is changing in recent years; for example, American food and drug legislation demands that the most sensitive individual be considered.

Addressing Distributional Inequities

There are ways to overcome the inequities of weighing the overall risk against risk to individuals. If a polluting electricity generating station is built it clearly provides benefit to everyone within its service range of perhaps 200 miles. Yet many risks are borne primarily by the neighbors, the most immediate of whom, those in the local city or township, are often compensated by a reduction in the local tax rate. As facilities are enlarged and the widespread nature of air pollution is more acutely perceived by citizens, the practical necessity of compensating citizens over a wider area than a local township becomes apparent.

In simpler cases almost all the risk is borne by one group, and that group also experiences the benefit. An especially simple case is that of the risk of cancer from hair dyes, where the group is just one individual who both bears the risk and reaps the benefits and to whom, moreover, the risk is voluntary. In such a case the main risk/benefit decision is a personal one, made by each and every person who uses the dye. The interest and duty of society is primarily to provide the information with which individuals can most satisfactorily make a decision.

In general, the level of aggregation of risks, costs, and benefits should be determined by the decision. National aggregation does not greatly assist a local decision maker.

Developing Decision Criteria

The risk/benefit assessor can suggest and outline logical procedures for making the final decision, guided by the preferences of the decision makers and any affected interest groups. A preference for avoidance of a very bad outcome such as a nuclear reactor accident or a dam failure would probably lead to decision criteria different from those suggested by a preference for maximizing the net benefit or expected value for such favorable outcomes as reduction of air pollution or reduction of poverty by cheap electricity.

Communicating and Summarizing the Analysis

The summary is often the only part of the analysis that is read. Various levels of summary are useful, but what is needed is a simple summary that expresses the range of possible outcomes. Because numbers and conclusions are likely to be quoted out of context by readers of the summary, the assumptions and limitations attached to them must be repeated, with reference made to the greater detail in the body of the report. Similarly, it is important that to any numbers error estimates be attached.

The possible a priori positions of a reader or decision maker must be included in the range of issues discussed. Readers disagreeing with the results will find it hard to condemn the calculation itself if their a priori positions have been clearly discussed. A successful analysis is one that elicits debate and criticism of its components rather than of its general methodology and one that forces critics into analysis of their own as well as the analyst's assumptions and methods.

The most important feature of a risk/benefit analysis is not the result itself but the logical procedure leading to it. Only when numbers and statements of the uncertainties are assigned at every stage can we be assured that the analyst has thought through the problem and so be assured that decisions are taken with the least uncertainty. Disagreement with such well-founded decisions will then be due to differences of opinion, and it should be possible to pinpoint where these differences exist.

CASE STUDIES

CASE 1: SACCHARIN

- *Source*: "Saccharin and Its Salts: Proposed Rule and Hearing," *Federal Register* 42 FR 19996 (Friday, April 15, 1977).

- *Original context*: Supplemental information provided with a proposed ruling by the Food and Drug Administration (FDA) of the U.S. Department of Health, Education, and Welfare.

- *Purpose*: The information is supplied to explain reasons for a proposed rule banning the use of saccharin as a food additive and expediting its evaluation for use as a single purpose drug available without prescription.

- *Subject matter*: The history of the use of saccharin and a description of safety tests performed on it and their relation to standard types of testing for identifying health risks are given. Fairly detailed descriptions are included of carcinogenicity tests performed and the significance of their results. A clear discussion of the necessity of and methods adopted in extrapolation of the results of testing food additives at high doses in animals to the presumed effects at low doses in man is included.

- *Risks included*: The main risk considered is that of induction of cancers in human beings from continued use of saccharin, although acute and chronic toxic effects are also mentioned.

- *Costs and benefits included*: The rule-making process for food additives does not require any considerations of costs or benefits, and none are included. For use in drugs, however, a balancing of risk and benefit is required. Although this is mentioned, no explicit quantification is attempted of either costs or benefits.

Summary

By 1976, use of saccharin was widespread. Over 70 percent of the 6–7.6 million pounds per year used in the United States was used in foods and beverages destined for human consumption, with additional uses in drugs and cosmetics and limited use in animal feed and drugs. Various reviews had been made of all information available on the toxicity of saccharin, the conclusion generally being that, in the quantities used, the health hazard from toxic effects was negligible, although it was noted that the studies performed to detect carcinogenicity were not as sensitive as modern standards would require. The continuing question about the carcinogenicity of saccharin and concern with its widespread and increasing use had led to the FDA's removal of it from the GRAS (generally recognized as safe) list in 1972 in an attempt to inhibit an increase in use by the general population. Since that time the results of several animal studies had become available, leading to the proposed ruling, because saccharin had been found to be a carcinogen, albeit a weak one, in rats.

Evaluating the carcinogenic effects of materials on human beings is highly problematic. The first association between occupational exposure (to soot) and cancer was made 200 years ago, but only much more recently did systematic study begin. The task is made difficult by many facts: Although cancer may be caused by many materials, not all persons exposed to the same material are affected; even potent carcinogens may require large fractions of a lifetime to make their effects known; there is little or no evidence of change before a cancer appears; laboratory tests are not necessarily conclusive; strong carcinogens are likely to be found rapidly, so the problem is the detection of weak ones.

The primary method of testing for chronic and acute effects is the use of long-term animal studies. Acceptable tests require the use of more than one animal species, continuation of the test throughout the lifetime of the animal, use of the highest doses feasible (the maximum tolerated without too great a weight loss or other major effects), sufficient numbers of animals, administration of the test material by a route similar to that by which human beings might be exposed, and, wherever possible, commencing exposure in utero.

It must be recognized that with the small number of animals (100 per species) that can be practically used in laboratory experiments, a negative result with doses close to the expected doses to be received by human beings would have little significance, since even as low a lifetime incidence of cancer as 10 percent would be close to the limit of reproducibility in such an experiment, because of spontaneous cancers and the expected random fluctuations. This would far exceed any acceptable risk for human beings, for whom in a population of 200 million, as in the United States, a cancer incidence of even 0.01 percent represents 20,000 cancers. It is thus necessary to administer very large doses to the small group of animals and to extrapolate the results to estimate the effects of lower doses while remembering that even then a negative result establishes only an upper bound to the risk and does not prove the noncarcinogenicity of the material tested.

Several methods of extrapolation have been proposed. Based on present knowledge the FDA believes the proper conservative approach is to assume a direct proportionality between the size of the dose and the incidence of tumors. Thus, if a daily dose of 1 gram of material per kilogram of bodyweight fed to experimental animals for a lifetime ($\sim$ 2 years for rats and mice) produces a 10 percent excess incidence of cancer, the FDA would assume that 0.1 grams per kilogram per day would give 1 percent tumor incidence, 0.01 gram per kilogram per day would give 0.1 percent incidence, and so on.

The results of several experiments on rats show that saccharin causes bladder tumors, the conclusive evidence being provided by a Canadian study that eliminated the possible effect of a contaminant of the saccharin used in previous attempts. In that study, a 24 percent incidence (twelve out of fifty) was noted in the most sensitive group of animals fed 5 percent saccharin in their diet, corresponding to about 2,500 milligrams/kilogram/day. Although a 24 percent incidence was noted, it is possible that this would have been different in a different set of animals. However, if it is assumed that the only differences are statistical fluctuations, because of the small numbers used, one may calculate that with 95 percent confidence the true effect of this dose level is less than 36 percent incidence.

These results of the animal tests can be extrapolated to low doses for the rats tested by using the assumption of proportionality. To apply the results to human beings, it is necessary to assume some relation between the sensitivity of rats and that of people to the carcinogen. One method is to assume that human sensitivity over a lifetime (seventy years) is equivalent to rats' sensitivity over a lifetime (two years for rats). The FDA went along with the opinion of most experts that this assumption is applicable, at least in the case of saccharin (which is hardly, if at all, metabolized in either rats or humans), so that the lifetime risk estimates for rats are directly applicable to human beings. On this basis, since 2.5 milligrams/kilogram/day (1/1,000 of the dose used in the experiment) may give up to 0.036 percent (about four in 10,000) lifetime tumor incidence, it follows that a human consumption of 150 milligrams/day (2.5 milligrams/kilogram/day × 60 kilograms weight) would give a similar lifetime incidence of four in 10,000 bladder cancers, which may be compared with the lifetime risk of bladder cancers in the United States of 100 in 10,000 without saccharin. (The risk of death is half this, since the long term survival is about fifty percent.) At the rate of four in 10,000 in a lifetime, if everybody in the United States consumed 150 milligrams/day, the annual cancer incidence due to saccharin consumption would be, assuming an average 70-year lifetime, less than 1,200 per year.

The three human epidemiological surveys mentioned in the FDA report were all too small in sample size to be sufficiently sensitive to detect such small increases in risk even though there exists a subpopulation (diabetics) who consume more than the usual amount of saccharin. Moreover, because of the possible long latent period of cancers (five to thirty years), it is possible that any effects of saccharin consumption were not yet apparent in any of these studies.

In addition to considering the use of saccharin in foods and beverages the FDA had to decide on its acceptability as an inactive ingredient in drugs and as a single-ingredient drug. In the first case, because saccharin was added as an inactive ingredient producing no direct therapeutic benefit and, moreover, because individuals had no choice to avert any risk from saccharin if it remained as an inactive ingredient, it was concluded that the risk of such use was not outweighed by the benefits and should cease. That is, in the future, drug manufacturers would have to demonstrate benefits outweighing the risks before they could include saccharin as an ingredient in any drug.

As a single-ingredient drug and the only nonnutritive sweetener on the market, saccharin might have some value for individuals who must control their intake of nutritive sweeteners, so that it might be marketable as a drug even though unsuitable as a food additive. The proper context for considering such use would be reviewal of a "new drug" application under the drug laws. If saccharin was approved as a single-ingredient drug, it would be suitable for over-the-counter (OTC), or nonprescription, use because of its lack of toxicity (except for the cancer risk, for which it would be labeled), the lack of any collateral measures for its safe use, and its long history of safe OTC use. However the obvious proposal leads to legal difficulties. To be registered as a drug, saccharin must be shown to be effective; the questions arise, "Effective for what?" and "What evidence is there?"

Many of the uses of saccharin in cosmetics result in a possible ingestion of saccharin. Despite the fact that the quantities of saccharin in these applications are small, the FDA considered that the use of saccharin affords no benefit sufficient to warrant any increased risk, so such uses should be banned. Similarly, use in animal drugs or feed requires demonstration of no residue in human food products; in the absence of such demonstration the FDA proposed that such use be banned and that use in non–food-producing animals provides no measurable benefit to outweigh the risks and so should also be discontinued.

Conclusions of the Study

The conclusions of the FDA and the basis of the proposed ruling are that saccharin is not safe for human consumption and does cause cancer in laboratory animals and thus may not be approved for continued use as a food additive. The FDA commissioner notes that he is acting under both the general safety requirement of the Food Additives Amendment of 1958 and the Delaney amendment to the Food, Drug, and Cosmetic Act, which states unequivocally that "[N]o additive shall be deemed to be safe if it is found to induce cancer when ingested by man or animal, or if it is found, after tests which are appropriate for the evaluation of the safety of food additives, to induce cancer in man or animal. . . . "

Analysis

Objective.   The objective of the supplemental information section of the proposed ruling with which we are concerned is to indicate the reasons for the proposed rules—rules that amount to the banning of the use of saccharin except possibly as a single-ingredient drug. It should be emphasized at the outset that the food laws under which this action was to be taken require that any food additive must be found to be safe for human consumption before it may be approved or, for those already approved, so that it may continue to be used and, further, that no additive that induces cancer (under appropriate conditions) may be approved. There is some leeway in the law for unintentional food additives, those entering the food chain by accident and in very small quantities. No one has suggested that the use of saccharin is not intentional, of course. In neither case was any allowance to be made for any possible benefit accruing through use of the additive in question. Thus in no sense is the major part of the material to be interpreted as a risk/cost/benefit study, but the case is included here because it provides a good example of the analysis of risk.

Assumptions. Assumptions of the risk analysis are clearly stated throughout the study.

Risks. The analysis of risks to human beings from ingestion of saccharin are clearly and logically stated and computed. Effects other than cancer are accepted as being negligible at any doses likely to be ingested by human beings, so the only risk treated in detail is that of cancer.

The history of the increasing use of saccharin and continuing uncertainty about its safety indicate a reason for concern. A short history of the scientific and medical inquiry into causes of cancer indicates that chemicals have definitely been associated with cancer induction and introduces the use of animal studies in testing of chemicals for carcinogenicity, detailing some of the protocols now considered necessary in such experiments. The necessity for extrapolation from large to low doses is explained, and an approach, direct proportionality, is adopted that is generally accepted as conservative, that is, it overestimates risks.

The results of actual experiments on animals are discussed, and it is concluded "unequivocally that saccharin causes bladder tumors in the test animals." This finding is then applied to the estimation of human risk, using stated assumptions. Assumed is direct proportionality between dose (in milligrams per kilogram per day) and cancer incidence, the lifetime probability of cancer due to saccharin consumption; also assumed is that, at least for saccharin, the lifetime risk for man is the same as for rat at the same dose (in milligrams per kilogram per day). A value for this risk is obtained by taking the 95 percent confidence upper bound on the largest risk observed in any group of rats tested. On this basis the lifetime risk to human beings ingesting 150 milligrams/day of saccharin (as in one large diet drink) could be as high as four parts in 10,000 (compared to a background of 100 per 10,000 for the type of cancer expected). In other terms this gives fewer than 1,200 persons per year dying of bladder cancer in the United States if all Americans ingested 150 milligrams/day of saccharin for life. (This corresponds to an annual U.S. saccharin consumption of 24 million pounds for food and beverages, compared with 1976 consumption of 6–7.6 million pounds, of which over 70 percent was for food and beverages although some of the other 30 percent may have resulted in human ingestion.)

The assumption made earlier, that the cancer incidence is proportional to dose, has the corollary that the total number of cancers caused in the population depends only on the total dose delivered to that population, provided the dose is spread out sufficiently but not necessarily uniformly. Thus continued consumption of 7 million pounds of saccharin per year (the 1976 figure) would eventually lead to an average of fewer than 400 deaths per year due to bladder cancer, compared to about 20 times that number dying of bladder cancer from other causes. It is evident that epidemiological surveys of human beings are unlikely to detect such a small effect, because the increase in lifetime risk is less than 5 percent (although in certain subpopulations of heavy consumers of saccharin the effect may be larger), for such surveys usually can detect risk increases only of order 100 percent or more.

Some scientists argue that the numerical relation between carcinogenicity in animal and in man is so imprecise as to be useless and that if a chemical is carcinogenic in animals it is probably carcinogenic in man but could have a high potency. They might argue that as many as 20 percent of all bladder cancers are now due to saccharin. This number is substantially bigger than suggested by the animal tests but still small enough that it would not have been detected in the epidemiological studies. In view of this it is explained by the FDA that the negative findings of three epidemiological studies among human beings do not contradict the animal studies.

Given this clear demonstration of risk of cancer, both the general safety requirements and the cancer agent requirement of the Delaney clause for food additives made the FDA's banning saccharin mandatory. However, recognizing the political effects of the decision, the FDA put in a delay that allowed Congress time to pass legislation explicitly exempting saccharin from these requirements.

Benefits. As mentioned earlier, when the risk of food additives is analyzed no account is taken of any benefits. For the additive's use in drugs and cosmetics some account of benefits should be taken, but no quantitative estimates are made in the FDA study in this respect, it being merely stated that for cosmetics no benefit sufficient to justify the risks exists, whereas drugs should be considered on a case-by-case basis.

In the discussion of saccharin use subsequent to the FDA's report, there has been little firm evidence that saccharin has any real benefit at all. The number of Americans who are overweight did not go down as saccharin consumption (or cyclamate consumption before 1970) went up (American Council on Science and Health 1978). The per capita sugar consumption has stayed high. It seems that the benefit, if any, is a benefit of personal pleasure. This benefit also accrues to the user of sweetened toothpaste, with a miniscule risk because of the small quantity.

A discussion has been made by Cohen (1978) of the comparative risk (due to carcinogenesis) of using saccharin and risk (due to overweight) of using sugar. This comparison is only part of the issue, for there are at least two other alternatives—using no sweetener or using some other nonnutritive sweetener (although none are currently on the market, it is possible that such alternatives pose less risk than saccharin). The saccharin issue, because it is of a type that can be easily understood, because saccharin is not very dangerous, and because saccharin use is widespread, is likely to be a landmark in risk comparison.

Uncertainties. Throughout the FDA's discussion uncertainties are considered, but no attempt is made to estimate their magnitude. Instead, procedures are adopted that are considered conservative in that they presumably overstate the risks. Examples include the use of the direct proportionality extrapolation from high to low doses and the use of the largest observed risk among all rat groups, increased by a factor of 3/2. (This would give a 95 percent confidence upper bound if there were only one observed group of rats. In fact, more groups were observed, and a correct statistical treatment would take account of all the observations.) One exception is the extrapolation from rats to human beings, on which there is little information, but the arguments given for adopting the assumption of equal risk for equal doses (in milligrams per kilogram per day) and some external evidence suggest that any error introduced by this procedure is less than a factor of 10.

Aggregation of Risks, Costs, and Benefits.   Because no benefits or costs are estimated, aggregation is not applicable.

Distribution of Risks, Costs, and Benefits.   No estimates are made of how the risks or any costs or benefits are distributed, the only estimate of risk referring to the entire population. It is evident, however, that risks are not uniformly distributed—the larger the dose of saccharin, the larger the risk. In addition, it is possible that some segments of the population (children, for example) may have higher sensitivity than others.

The Use Made of the Risk Study

It is clear that the small size of the risk and the widespread use of saccharin make the saccharin issue of unusually widespread concern to Americans. Some of the American people seem to have been angry at the FDA commissioner for proposing to ban saccharin. Yet he is constantly urged to take action to ban, and has banned, accidental food additives that on the same conditional basis would give cancer to only one or two persons a year. To ignore a death rate of 1,200 per year would be illogical, and even to postpone action, as he did, awaiting congressional discussion was inconsistent.

Congress passed a law preventing action on the saccharin case for a year and demanding warning labels in every store selling products containing saccharin. In this time Congress hoped that a safe substitute could be found. At the time of writing (April 1981) this law had expired, but a further law suspending regulation until December 1982 was before Congress. In the meantime, although the Food and Drug Administration appears to have a duty to regulate the sale of saccharin, no action is being taken. Despite congressional hearings, a National Academy of Sciences study, and private studies, opinion remains divided. Many would put no restrictions on saccharin, or at least only minor labeling restrictions, while others support the original FDA proposal, although few support a complete ban.

CASE 2: ACCIDENT RISKS IN NUCLEAR
POWER PLANTS

- *Source*: Nuclear Regulatory Commission. 1975. "Reactor Safety Study: An Assessment of Accident Risks in U.S. Commercial Nuclear Power Plants," NUREG 75/014, WASH–1400.

- *Original context*: A report with executive summary and eleven appendices, issued in draft in 1974 and in final form after public comment one year later.

- *Purpose*: The principal objective of the study is to reach some meaningful conclusions about the risk of nuclear accidents using then current technology. It is recognized that the current state of knowledge would probably not permit a complete analysis of low-probability accidents with the desired precision. The study proposes to consider the uncertainty in present knowledge and the consequent range in the predictions as well as delineating outstanding problems. In this way, any uncertainties in the results of the study can be placed in perspective. Then, although the results must be imprecise in some aspects, the study nevertheless can serve as an important first step in the development of quantitative risk analysis methods.

- *Subject matter*: Two nuclear reactors are analyzed, a pressurized water reactor (PWR) and a boiling water reactor (BWR). The specific plants chosen are the Surry Power Station (Unit 1, 788 megawatts electrical capacity, a PWR of Westinghouse design), and the Peach Bottom Atomic Power Station (Unit 2, 1,065 megawatts electrical capacity, a BWR of General Electric design). All event sequences (event trees) that might, in the opinion of the authors, lead to appreciable hazard to the general public are analyzed. In all, eighty-two event trees are believed to be significant for the PWR and a similar number for the BWR.

- *Risks included*: The risks included are immediate death (within a week) from radiation and delayed, or latent, cancer deaths.

- *Costs included*: No costs are assessed.

- *Benefits included*: The benefit of electricity from nuclear power is implied but not explicitly stated.

Summary of Methodology

The observation is made that only in the event of melting of the reactor fuel (a meltdown) would enough radioactivity be released to cause a major hazard to the public. The fuel consists of sintered pellets of the ceramic uranium dioxide packed in zirconium alloy (zirc-alloy) tubes.

A set of accident sequences, or event trees, is postulated that lead to a meltdown. The event trees are chosen so that the probability of an event at each branch is approximately independent of the choice at other branches.

The probability of failure of a safety system at a branch is estimated by means of a fault tree using known or estimated data on failure of components, including, where appropriate, random failure in human responses (but see the later comment on correlated failure of human response).

Using the results of the probability estimates as applied to the event trees, the probability of a meltdown is calculated as

$$P = \prod_i p_i \quad ,$$

where p_i is the probability of failure at the branch i.

The consequences of a meltdown are assumed to be independent of the cause of the meltdown, except that the time of meltdown, which determines the radioactivity available for release, varies in different cases. The probability of failure of the containment vessel is estimated from engineering judgment; the probability of dispersion of radioactivity is calculated assuming measured weather conditions for the assumed sites.

The prompt effect of radioactivity on the population is estimated primarily from the data summarized in the report by the Committee on the Biological Effects of Ionizing Radiation (BEIR I) of the National Academy of Sciences (NAS) and National Research Council (NAS 1972). For latent cancers, animal data are used that suggest that at low dose rates the effect is one-quarter of the effect suggested by BEIR I.

Conclusions of the Study

The results are presented in integral plots of annual probability of the number of immediate deaths exceeding a number x, a probability for latent cancers exceeding a number y, and probability of genetic effects, thyroid diseases, and property damage, all computed on the assumption of 100 operating reactors of the type studied. These results show that there is a probability of about 10^{-8} per reactor year of an accident with 3,000 acute fatalities and 60,000 latent cancers.

In order to put these numbers into perspective they are compared with risks for several other manmade accidents—aircraft crashes, fires, explosions, and chlorine leaks—and also with risks for some natural hazards—meteor, hurricanes, tornadoes, and earthquakes. No attempt was made to carry out a risk/benefit calculation.

Analysis

This report on nuclear accident risk has been more widely discussed and criticized than almost any other. In particular, a committee (Lewis et al. 1978) set up by the Nuclear Regulatory Commission (NRC) at the request of Congress reviewed it.

Objective.   The stated objective of the report was to be a first step in the development of quantitative risk analysis methods. This it was, as Lewis observed, since:

The study was an essential first step beyond earlier attempts to estimate the risks of nuclear power,

The study attained a high level of objectivity in safety assessment by introducing a workable accident classification and by presenting a methodology for the quantitative determination of risk,

The use of event trees and failure trees together with an adequate data base has proved to be the best available tool for the quantification of the probability of occurrence of accidents,

The importance of latent fatalities and property damage was recognized besides that of immediate fatalities.

Assumptions. The report, while comprehensive, is not easy to read and the assumptions are not easy to find. The basic assumption in setting up the event trees, that the probabilities are independent, is not clearly brought out. Nor is it clearly stated that the results depend on the belief that all important event trees have been considered. There can be no proof of this, but, if as time goes on no more event trees are found, it appears likely. As stressed by Lewis, some events (sabotage, earthquakes, fires) do not lend themselves to event tree analysis and must be added separately. The assumption has been widely criticized that in analyzing one accident sequence, called *anticipated transient without scram* (ATWS), in a boiling water reactor, the probability of failure to insert enough control rods is calculable from probabilities of individual control rod failures. Such a failure may arise from a single physical cause rather than a set of independent causes affecting individual control rods—that is, it may be a common mode failure.

Risks are calculated for those events that could be modeled by an event tree, but only qualitative discussion was made of fires, earthquakes, and sabotage. Benefits are not calculated.

Uncertainties. Uncertainties are estimated for the probability at each branch of the event trees and were aggregated using a Monte Carlo method. The uncertainties in the probability of an accident and in the consequences are separately stated. They are not combined although they could have been. Lewis et al. (1978) believe that these uncertainties are understated and that reactors could be either safer or less safe than claimed by the report. The uncertainties are probably dominated by the event trees not included and by events such as sabotage that are not amenable to this analysis.

Aggregation and Distribution. The aggregation of and the discussion of distribution of risks is not well done. The authors chose to present an average and not to calculate separately the risk for each reactor or each population group. The risk is certainly greater for someone near a reactor than for someone farther away. The authors of the study chose to present the risk to society as a whole from 100 reactors in typical sites.

Extensions

Although not explicitly stated, the study applies to reactors as designed before and operated by 1974 and does not apply to reactors of designs other than those of General Electric and Westinghouse. The study has been overly praised by nuclear industry advocates and overly damned by critics but has not been used to ensure safety. Indeed, if the methods had been applied to Babcock & Wilcox reactors, many observers believe that defects would have been observed and that the Three Mile Island accident would have been avoided.

The event tree analysis can be used in design and licensing. For any new light water reactor, for example, the questions can be asked: How do the eighty-two event trees apply to the new reactor? Are the probabilities greater or smaller? Have any design changes increased the importance of any hitherto ignored event tree? To the extent that operator error contributes to a failure, can these event trees be used in operator training to assure proper response? In the event of a severe accident, does the study suggest mitigating methods, such as evacuation, to reduce the overall number of cancers? This use of the methodology of the reactor safety study has been urged by many authors, especially Lewis et al. (1978) and Kemeny et al. (1979).

The study uses for comparison other accidents, both natural and manmade, but no direct comparisons with other energy supply options. The latter would enable us to compare one risk with another for the same benefit (electricity). Note that this might involve comparing risks of different types, differently calculated (as discussed in Chapter 2), which might and probably should be perceived differently.

The use of this methodology to improve safety is widely touted as independent of the absolute accuracy of the risk calculation. But some idea of the absolute accuracy is required to allow comparison with other risk/benefit analyses and thus to permit understanding at what point further reductions of risk would be out of proportion in cost effectiveness.

An extension of the methodology to siting of reactors, either to choose an acceptable site or to choose an optimum site, is straightforward and is under way. Also under way is extension to choice of the best actions to take when an accident occurs—whether or how much to evacuate, whether to administer thyroid blocking agents to prevent uptake of radioactive iodine, and so forth.

CASE 3:   AUTOMOBILE SAFETY FEATURES

- *Source*:   Lave, B.L., and W.E. Weber. 1970. "A Benefit-Cost Analysis of Auto Safety Features." *Applied Economics* 2, No. 4: 265–275.

- *Purpose*:   "[T]o provide an individual with information to enable him to decide whether he should purchase particular safety features."

- *Subject matter*:   Padded instrument panels, dual braking systems, collapsible steering columns, and seat belts.

- *Risks included*:   Death, dangerous injury, nondangerous injury, and minor injuries.

- *Costs included*:   Extra costs of the four safety devices.

- *Benefits included*:   Benefits are not calculated in the analysis. Instead, as described below, the risks and costs are used to evaluate a dollar value which is the breakeven value for a parameter representing an individual's demand for safety.

- *Alternatives considered*:   None.

Summary of Methodology

The authors compute the risks (probability per automobile per year) of the various categories of injuries from death statistics and single point estimates of injuries in one year, 1965. The estimates are based on a sample of rural injury-producing accidents.

Single point estimates are made of the efficacy of the safety devices. Dual brakes are assumed to prevent all accidents associated with defective brakes. The efficacy of padded instrument panels and of seat belts in reducing the risks of the various injury categories is estimated by interpreting the results of other studies, while that of collapsible steering columns is estimated from photographs and descriptions of twenty-eight fatal accidents in which the driver was killed by impact with a noncollapsible column.

Using the estimated efficacies and the computed risks, the risk reduction is computed (100 percent usage of seat belts is assumed). The authors then make "reasonable" assumptions about the costs of the safety devices.

An interest rate is assumed for discounting over the (assumed six-year) life of an automobile. Five rates are used in the computations, to cover a range of possibilities.

A weighting factor is assigned to each category of injury (and death) to account for an individual's different averseness for each. Six different sets of weights are used in the computations to give some idea of the possible variations resulting from different weighting.

A parameter b is defined as the "implied amount that an individual would be willing to pay to avert death in a given year." It is "implied" because it is defined as 5,000 times how much per car each individual would be willing to pay to lower the probability of a death occurring in that car during one year from four in 10,000 to two in 10,000. This parameter was mentioned previously under Benefits. With the assumption of linearity between risk aversion and the amount that would willingly be paid, the indifference values of b under the various assumptions made are computed as the values of b at which

$$ z = b \sum_{r=1}^{6} \frac{1}{(1+i)^r} \, \mathbf{w} \cdot \mathbf{x} \quad , $$

where z = the cost of the safety feature.
$\mathbf{w}$ = a vector of weights for injury types.
$\mathbf{x}$ = a vector of risk reduction for injury types.
i = the interest rate.

Tables are presented for each safety feature giving the indifference values of b for the five interest rates and six weighting schemes considered.

Conclusions of the Study

The main results of the study are presented in the tables of break-even values for the "demand for safety" parameter, which show under the conditions assumed that the best safety features are seat belts, followed in order by collapsible steering columns, padded instrument panels, and finally dual-braking systems. It is then stated as a general conclusion, that the "average consumer was probably correct in choosing not to purchase dual braking systems, padded instrument panels and collapsible steering columns; if he did not intend to use them most of the time, he was correct in not purchasing seat belts," with the qualification that "correct" assumes that the demand for safety is equal to the median family income.

Analysis

Objective. The sole objective of the paper is that listed previously under "Purpose," although the authors suggest that their conclusions should "cause one to question the wisdom of requiring these safety features" on new automobiles. (See discussion later.)

Assumptions. Although most of the study's assumptions are clearly stated, some remain implicit that are important for any attempt at a risk/benefit analysis for individuals. The most important is that the risk is the same for all individuals (actually, for all automobiles, because the average risk is calculated per automobile), independent of the type or size of vehicle, the annual mileage, geographic area, and individual driving patterns. Although such an assumption should be valid for a societywide risk/benefit analysis, the neglected parameters must be taken into account in assessment of risk to any individual.

Risks. Given the assumptions, the risks of the various injury categories, and the reductions in risk associated with the four safety features are clearly and simply calculated.

Benefits. The benefits of the safety features are not calculated, except insofar as the calculated reductions in risks may be considered as benefits. Presumably, if it is assumed that property damage is unchanged—that accident rates and severities remain unchanged except for the reduction in amount of injury—on the introduction of the safety measures, various monetary benefits can be expected to accrue. Not only would the individual user of the safety devices be likely to benefit, because of lower medical bills in the event of accident (although it is possible they could increase if accidents that would have been fatal without the safety devices resulted in serious injury with the devices) but also to society as a whole, because of possible reduction in resources devoted to medical care and retention of the investment in training of the individual, to name just two benefits. The methodology adopted in the study does not require the computation of any such benefits, although the individual's estimate of parameter b implicitly measures that individual's perception of his or her probable benefits.

Uncertainties.   Any study such as this is evidently subject to major uncertainties. Although the authors state that they would only "spend little time defending the particular estimates [they] have derived," they make no attempt to list or quantify the uncertainties, and indeed, some of the figures in their tables are quoted to absurd accuracy (amounts in dollars given to seven places in one table, where only the first one or two places are actually significant). Let us here outline some of the areas in which the uncertainties lie. Some of these we have already suggested in the section "Assumptions"; variation of any of the implicit assumptions mentioned there will give rise to large variations in the risk reductions obtained with each safety device. For example, the figures used for accident risk are nationwide averages and so are appropriate for calculating the societal, rather than individual, reductions in risk. For individuals it might be more appropriate to use the risk per vehicle mile traveled, and then scale all the results with the individual's annual mileage. Similarly, geographical variation should be included, together with variations with type and size of automobile.

In addition to these uncertainties, the authors discuss at length the inherent difficulties in evaluating the efficacy of the safety devices but make no attempt to indicate the effect on their conclusions of differing estimates of these efficacies. In view of the small size, nonrandomness, and occasional lack of objectivity in estimation, considerable error may be expected.

As a final example of the uncertainties of the study, the figures used for the costs of the safety features are merely guesses made by the authors, who argue that they are "in the ball park." The actual costs may vary substantially from those quoted, and the relative costs for the different features could be drastically different. Variation of the former would proportionately affect the absolute values of the break-even values of b (see "Summary of Methodology"), and variation of the latter might affect the "value-for-money" ordering of the safety features.

Aggregation and Distribution of Risks and Benefits. Since benefits were not estimated in the study, no attempt was made to aggregate risks and benefits, although the various risks actually considered were combined into a single numerical measure by the use of weighting factors, a range of which was examined.

Distribution of Risks and Benefits. The distribution of possible risks and benefits was not discussed at all, the explicit purpose of the study being to estimate the worths of the various safety features to the owner of the car only. It should be noted, however, that automobile accidents often involve more than just the owners of the vehicles involved. There is also, for example, the cost to society of maintaining rescue and hospital equipment and personnel. Ideally, of course, such costs would be factored into each automobile owner's estimate of the worth of reduction of risk, but unless explicitly included, they are unlikely to be fully accounted for.

Extensions

At several places in the analysis extensions are in order. The main points of the article was to provide a methodology for individual decisions, but it failed to take into account the many individual variations needed (for example, those mentioned under "Assumptions"). We therefore suggest two lines along which a fuller analysis might proceed. First, for an individual, the extra factors mentioned could be included. Second, for society as a whole, such extra factors mentioned are not necessary, and nationwide (for example) averages could be taken, but the effective benefit—the value of the risk reduction—would need much closer analysis.

The analysis failed to include a second-order effect. Does the possession of a safety feature such as a seat belt make the driver less careful, in the way that a roll bar on a racing car might encourage him to drive faster, or more careful, in that he thinks of safety as he buckles his seat belt?

CASE 4: RADIATION EXPOSURE

- *Source*: Terrill, J.G. 1972. "Cost-Benefit Estimates for the Major Sources of Radiation Exposure." *American Journal of Public Health* 62 (July): 1008–1013.

- *Original context*: Originally presented at the 99th Meeting of the American Public Health Association.

- *Purpose*: "To make a cost benefit analysis of two of the more important sources of radiation exposure . . . i.e. the radiation generated by nuclear power plants and that generated by medical x-ray machines."

- *Subject matter*: The article attempts to estimate the cost of reducing population exposure to ionizing radiation arising from two of the more important man-made sources—X-ray machines, which contribute more than 90 percent of human exposure from such sources, and nuclear power plants, which contribute less than 1 percent. In the case of X-ray machines, the measures assessed are now required at least in new equipment, whereas the estimates for nuclear power plants were hypothetical at the time the article was written.

- *Risks included*: In each case the only risk assessed is the magnitude of the total correctable radiation dose to the gonads of persons exposed, expressed in man-rem. It is assumed that this is a consistent measure of the risk from both sources, and so no conversion to any other measure is attempted.

- *Costs included*: Estimates of the extra costs of equipment for both X-ray machines and nuclear power plants are the only costs considered.

- *Benefits included*: The only benefit included is the implied reduction in risk through reduction in radiation exposure.

Summary of Methodology

The total American population's exposure to X rays was estimated by surveys carried out for the Bureau of Radiological Health of the

U.S. Public Health Service in 1964 and again in 1970. The results of these surveys allow estimation of average gonadal dose per X-ray exposure for males and females and for X-ray machines in different locations (hospitals, physicians' offices, and dental offices are mentioned in the article), together with numbers of persons X-rayed, numbers of X-ray visists, and numbers of examinations. Using this information the author computes the total gonadal exposure from X-ray machines to the whole population of the United States and hence the exposure per X-ray machine. The authors of the 1970 report for the Bureau of Radiological Health also estimated that an average of 65 percent of this exposure was correctible—that it fulfilled no useful purpose and could have been avoided by collimating the X-ray beam to prevent irradiation of the gonads—although the proportion varied with the type of machine and the care taken in its operation. For machines in hospitals, the correctable gonadal dose per year and per machine is computed from these data, the figures obtained being 160–320 man-rem per machine per year. Further Bureau of Radiological Health estimates of the cost of improving the collimation of the X-ray beam ($400–$2,000 per machine) are used to give an average cost for the reduction of exposure of $7 per man-rem per year.

The reduction in dose and the cost estimates for nuclear power plants are based on much less reliable data. Figures are presented showing total nonoccupational population exposure (whole body dose) per power reactor to be below 400 man-rem per year (an upper limit proposed by the Atomic Energy Commission and adopted as an upper limit design criterion by the NRC), the range being from 1 to 360 man-rem per year for five plants in 1969 (mean value ~ 100 man-rem). It is then assumed that an average of ~ 100 man-rem per year (for an average 1,000 MW(e) plant) represents a reasonable estimate of the correctable gonadal radiation exposure that might be achievable per nuclear power plant by using additional waste-handling facilities to achieve radiation release as low as practicable. Cost figures of from 10^6 to 10^7 per plant are assumed, on the basis of hardware commitments of manufacturers, to give cost figures for exposure reduction of 10^4 to 10^5 per man-rem per year, although the upper limit rises to $465,000 per man-rem per year if the actual total correctable exposure due to twenty plants (430 man-rem) operating in 1970 is used.

Conclusion of the Study

The conclusion is that resources spent to improve medical X-ray equipment represent a better value to citizens than resources spent on additional waste-handling facilities at nuclear power plants (by a factor of 1,000 to 60,000). An estimate of the average cost to patients of the improvements to X-ray machines is made by amortising the capital cost over ten years, which gives an additional cost of about 1¢ per X-ray film.

Analysis

Objective.   The stated objective of the article, a cost-benefit analysis, is not attempted. Instead, the analysis is based on the relative cost of reduction of a given risk (man-rem of exposure). Despite its inadequacies, it does give some idea of the relative costs, the factor of difference making the errors in analysis unimportant. It clearly indicates that for any reduction in population exposure to be achieved, the X-ray machine is the primary and most cost effective target.

It is unclear what relevance should be attached to the result. Analysis such as this is most useful if it is performed in order to clarify some decision just made or about to be made. Here no reference is made to any such decision, and the results must be considered of academic interest until they can be brought to bear in decision making.

Assumptions.   The overall plan of the article is clear, but some of the details of the assumptions are not. Most of the data refer to 1964 for the X-ray case, but various estimates are also made for the future (1980) although no information is given for the basis of any such extrapolations. It is also evident that either nomenclature varies between text and tables or there are inconsistencies between numbers given in the text and in the tables (by factors $\lesssim 2$). (In part, these inconsistencies may have resulted from the data's original presentation in a conference paper.)

Risks.   The risk calculated is the total correctable gonadal radiation exposure (in man-rem) for X-ray machines and the whole body (and hence gonadal) population exposure (nonoccupational) from nuclear reactors, the assumption being that each may be reduced. Under the conditions stated (1964 technology and practices) these exposures are clearly stated. It is interesting to note that under these conditions the correctable exposure per hospital X-ray machines was of the same order as the total exposure per nuclear power plant, although there are thousands of X-ray machines and fewer than 100 nuclear power plants in the United States. The bases of the extrapolation to the future were not made clear and are highly questionable, especially in view of legislation introduced even before the paper was presented.

No attempt is made to assess the risks, if any, of the actions under consideration—whether the addition of collimators in X-ray machines or the provision of extra waste treatment facilities on nuclear power plants would involve any extra risk for any segment of the population.

Benefits and Costs. The extra cost of adding collimators to X-ray machines is translated into a cost per X-ray film, but no similar attempt is made at estimating the extra cost of electricity at nuclear power plants. The only benefit that may be inferred is the reduction of risk associated with reduction in radiation exposure, but no estimates are made of any tangible effect of such radiation.

Uncertainties. The uncertainties in the figures presented in this study are not well demonstrated, although, as noted previously, because of the large ratio of cost-effectiveness between the two actions considered, such uncertainties are unlikely to alter the conclusions. In most cases where a range of values is given for any parameter, some undefined mean value is used for the analysis. The considerable uncertainties in the input data are not mentioned, and the even larger uncertainty in any possible extrapolations to the whole population considered—especially to future populations—are also given no consideration. Indeed, several of the tables in the paper have projections to 1980 of the expected dose from X-rays and nuclear power plants. No information is given on how such projections were arrived at, nor on the possible errors in such projections, especially in light of actions already taken to reduce exposure.

Aggregation of Risks and Benefits. No attempt is made to aggregate risks, benefits, and costs in order to compare their relative magnitudes. This is partly because the study was intended to compare only two specific actions on a cost-effectiveness basis and partly because the relative risks and so on are not presented.

Distribution of Risks and Benefits.   Again, no particular attempt is made to discuss the distribution of risks, benefits, and costs. It is implied, in the case of X-rays, that the cost would probably be met in some way by those receiving the benefit of reduction in exposure, in the form of an increased cost per X-ray film, but no equivalent estimate is made for the nuclear power plants.

Extensions

Many possible extensions of this study are apparent. The comparison being made is between the easiest portion of the reduction in exposure possible for X-ray machines and the hardest part for nuclear power plants, for the regulation of X-ray machines has been considerably less stringent than that for nuclear power plants. Indeed, the correctable X-ray exposure considered is already being reduced through comparatively cheap additions of collimators on all new X-ray machines. More useful, perhaps, would be an analysis of the risks, costs, and benefits for reduction of all "correctable" exposures (defined in the article as those not necessary for exposing the X-ray film) and also for the reduction of the "uncorrectable" exposure. That is, is it possible to reduce the exposure required to take X-ray films at all, and what are the risks, costs, and benefits of doing so? Risks analyzed should include those of fabrication of the machines, as well as any risks to operators and maintenance technicians together with the persons actually being X-rayed. In aggregating risks, benefits, and costs, the X-ray case is comparatively simple because most of the benefit and cost accrues to the persons being X-rayed, although society as a whole presumably obtains some benefit from a reduction in X-ray exposure through a reduction in cancers and genetic disorders. For the nuclear power plant, however, the task is more difficult. At the correction costs quoted in the article ($\sim \$10^6$ per nuclear power plant), there is a nonnegligible component of risk from the construction of the required facilities, which accrues to those doing the construction. Benefit due to reduction in exposure accrues mostly to those closest to the nuclear power plant, but also to society as a whole to some extent (as for X-rays). The cost is borne by the users of the electricity from the nuclear power plant (note that 10^6 per 1,000 MW(e) plant would add 0.5 percent to the cost of electricity).

No discussion is made of the possibility of reducing X-ray exposure by avoiding unnecessary X-rays or by postponing necessary X-rays to a more propitious time. It has been widely alleged, and it appears plausible, that many X-rays are taken to protect the physician from possible malpractice suits without regard to cost or risk. The benefit of the X-ray then accrues primarily to the physician, but the risk and the cost to the patient. Conversely, in such a case, the benefit of avoiding X-rays accrues to the patient and the risk (of a catastrophic lawsuit) to the physician.

CASE 5: NUCLEAR COPPER MINING

- *Source*: G.H. Higgins. 1972. "Benefits and Risks from Conventional and Nuclear Copper Mining." 10 pages, in *Risk vs. Benefit: Solution or Dream*, edited by H.J. Otway. LA–4860–MS, Los Alamos Scientific Laboratory.

- *Original context*: An informal report distributed by the National Technical Information Service.

- *Purpose*: A quantitative comparison of conventional and nuclear explosion stimulated copper production methods.

- *Subject matter*: Methods of conventional copper mining and an approach using nuclear explosions followed by leaching and electrowinning are discussed from the point of view of environmental risks. A dollar value is assigned to each risk to derive a total cost and hence a cost/benefit ratio.

- *Risks included*: From conventional mining, blast and ground shock from conventional explosive; sulfur dioxide emissions; silt-, copper-, and acid-bearing water from treatment; particulate emissions from grinding rock and from roads; aesthetics of tailings piles, mine facilities, and excavations; risk to mine operators. From nuclear mining, blast and ground shock from nuclear explosions; copper-, acid-, and tritium-bearing water from treatment; radiation from venting during or immediately after blast and from regular emissions of off gas.

- *Costs included*:   Not relevant, see descriptions.

- *Benefits included*:   All the risks are assigned dollar values and are then compared with the only assumed benefit, the market price of copper.

Summary of Methodology

The purpose of the study is to assign dollar values to the various risks associated with two methods of mining copper. These methods are, first, conventional mining, consisting of the process steps mining, milling, concentration, roasting-smelting, converting, anode casting, electro-refining and melting-casting, and second, nuclear stimulated mining with the postulated process steps of explosion shattering of the rock in situ, oxygen leaching again in situ, and electrowinning. No attempt is made to compare the economics of the methods, and only specific health and environmental risks are compared. It is emphasized in the study that the two methods are not alternatives at the same site, but it is also claimed that they are competitive in an economic sense.

For conventional mining the risks included are those we listed. Minor risks are not included. Costs are assigned to each risk, with data taken from other studies. The cost of the sulfur dioxide emissions is taken as $43 per ton, from a study by Lave and Seskin (1970) suggesting that a 50 percent reduction in SO_2 levels throughout the United States would result in a 10^9 reduction in health costs, and it is stated that this is likely to be a high estimate. It is retained only as being understood to include such direct health effects and also all other environmental effects. (No justification is provided for this opinion.) The cost of water pollution is estimated as $10 per acre-foot, on the basis that the value of the water (assuming control of it) is only the value of its temporary diversion, which may range from $5/acre-foot to $200/acre-foot, and that, in the case of nuclear mining, "It is assumed that deep ground water is used for processing and returned to the rubble column." The aesthetic cost of pits and tailings deposits is estimated by computing the cost to fill them in or remove them, respectively, although a figure 100 times higher is suggested as the possible cost if they are left for 100 years. For accidental death or permanent disability a value of $250,000 per death or disability is used, together with statistical data on the past history of copper mining. The overall result is a cost of the risks of conventional copper mining at \$72 to \$115 per ton of copper giving a benefit/risk ratio of 13.9 to 8.7, based on an assumed benefit equal to a market price of \$1,000/ton.

For nuclear mining the calculated risks are acknowledged to be far more uncertain, for every estimate has to be based on extrapolation, no copper having actually been mined by this process. Radiation risks arise from the possibility of venting at the time of the explosion, or later seepage of radioactive gases during leaching and at the time of first breakthrough during drilling into the radioactive zone, or during the leaching operation from gases bled off, or during electrowinning from the radionuclide contamination of the copper-bearing leach solution. The probability of venting is claimed to be "almost certainly" less than 1 in 1,000 per explosion. Weapons tests in the same yield range buried $350-400W^{1/3}$ feet deep (where W is the explosive yield in kilotons) experienced no prompt radioactive releases (although three seeped radioactive gases) in sixty-five test explosions, and it is assumed that deeper burial to $540W^{1/3}$ feet would reduce the risk of venting by a factor of at least 5. In the worst case, radiation doses from such venting were estimated to be less than 0.17 rem at all distances beyond 17 miles per 12,000 tons of copper recovered and 40 rem at 1 mile to a person spending his whole life at that distance.

The data base does not provide very stringent limits according to the study. To develop a 550×10^6 ton ore body, there would be approximately 100 detonations leading to less than a 1 in 10 chance of radiation exposure from venting. For drilling there are risks from bled off gases, principally Kr^{87}, Ar^{37}, and tritium (as tritiated water, HTO). The emissions are expected to be within present standards but will increase the worldwide burden of these gases. Within the processing buildings HTO vapor could reach 300 times 1971 permissible concentrations without process plant ventilation.

Probabilities are estimated for risks of property damage from ground shock effects. Of course, this would be site specific. For this hypothetical assessment it is assumed that only 1,000 people are resident within a radius of 50 miles, with a total of only 250 structures within that radius. No persons are assumed to live closer than 1 mile. Each item of architectural damage is assigned a cost of \$500 (\$50,000 for on-site equipment) for repair, but these direct costs are omitted from the calculations because they are assumed to be internalized (and met via insurance or direct repair), the relevant cost of such damage thus becoming just the nuisance value of it, rated at $50 per person-day. Environmental cost of radiation release, both accidental and planned, is taken to be $250 per person-rem (corresponding to $\sim \$10^6$ per death from cancer, assuming the BEIR I (1972) figure of $\sim 5{,}000$ person-rem per cancer).

Conclusion of the Study

The study concludes that in both methods the benefit (taken to be the market price of around $1,000 per ton) far exceeds the risk component of costs. The last are assessed at $72–115 per ton of copper for conventional mining and $5 per ton from nuclear mining, so that the latter method entails risks "surely no greater than from conventional copper mining, and probably an order of magnitude less."

Analysis

Objective.   The aim of the article is to make a quantitative comparison between the risks of conventional copper mining and a copper mining technique using nuclear explosions. From the very limited set of risks considered and the often cavalier method of treating them, this objective cannot be considered to have been met. Given some of the references cited it appears, although it is never explicitly stated, that this study may be a summary of more extensive unpublished work, but if so it is either not a good summary or else the broader work has the same flaws.

Assumptions.   Large numbers of assumptions made are not explicitly stated or, if stated, are not justified in any way. The major one is that the two methods are at least not too different in total economic cost. It is stated that a "similar comparison of the economics of the two methods has been performed," but we the readers are not informed of the outcome, so that we are implicitly left to assume that the costs are not too disparate, since sufficient expenditure would be able to reduce substantially most of the risks discussed.

Similarly, we are informed that minor risks are not considered, but the absence of any list of what were considered minor risks or even of a value attached to the total of all the minor risks makes one doubt whether much consideration was given to those risks not explicitly mentioned. It is clear, however, that in some instances, possible major risks were omitted (see subsequent discussion).

As another example of the lack of clarity of the assumptions, it is never stated what parts of the two methods are to be included as producing risks. This is exemplified by the treatment of seismic shock damage. Some crude estimates of the direct cost of repairing this damage are made (these estimates, at $11/ton copper/1,000 people living within 50 miles plus $4/ton copper damage to plant, are larger than the estimated total costs of all other risks for nuclear mining) but then ignored as being "internalized through seismic damage insurance or direct repair." The nuisance value of such damage is included though. Similar confusion appears over the cost of risk to employees. In the conventional mining case, taking a figure of 150 serious disabilities or deaths in the copper mining industry in the United States each year gives a risk per ton of copper of $\sim 8.7 \times 10^{-5}$ per year of death or serious disability, which is translated into a cost of $21.75 per ton, assuming a cost of $250,000 per case ("a rough average of jury awards in such cases"). In the nuclear mining case, only the risk due to radiation is assessed, other industrial accidents being omitted. Although copper mining is hazardous compared to an average of all occupations, the risk per employee does not differ greatly from other heavy industries, so that one would expect a significant number of industrial accidents in any nuclear industry also, and the cost of such risks is almost certain to be greater than that of any radiation hazards permitted.

Risks.   The only risks considered are those listed earlier, each being assigned a cost as described in the section "Summary of Methodology." A severe flaw in the study is the incorrect use of statistics to back up the author's argument on the probability of venting following an underground explosion. The observed datum that there have been no occurrences of venting in sixty-five nuclear weapons tests is used as support for the statement that the probability of venting is "almost certainly" less than 1 in 1,000. In fact, the 0/65 result gives the much less constraining 95 percent confidence limit that the probability is less than 45 in 1,000 (assuming a constant probability per explosion). Even allowing the factor 5 improvement postulated (on what basis is not specified) gives a 10 times higher estimate than allowed for, although even this higher estimate would make little difference (10 percent) in the final valuation of the risks, assuming the valuations are good estimates. Even so, one is left feeling wary over accepting on trust, as explicitly required by the author, other figures given in the articles. (Note that the author's estimate may be correct, but the evidence quoted as supportive does not in fact provide support.)

Risks dismissed as minor are not even enumerated. It is, for example, not clear that the cost of risks from tailings piles and pits is simply equal to the costs of removing or filling them in. No consideration has apparently been given to the high probability, and possibly high risk, of disruption and contamination of aquifers. Similarly disregarded were such effects in regions of rock fractured by the nuclear explosion, the effect on aquifers of the leaching solutions used, and the risk to future generations from the radioactive fission products remaining underground or the toxic elements mobilized by conventional mining techniques.

Also not treated or even mentioned is any risk inherent in the production and transport of the nuclear explosives. Although such risks may be minor, the possibility of theft of what amounts to nuclear weapons used in an industrial setting at least deserves some mention.

The risks stemming directly from the process involved are usually the most important. But in the case of nuclear explosives there may well be secondary risks that outweigh the direct risks in importance: Proliferation of nuclear explosives could lead to a proliferation of nuclear weapons, which might destabilize the international scene and increase the chance of war.

Although these risks are hard to discuss and very uncertain, their importance is unquestioned and omission of any discussion brings discredit on the study, for it is not unlikely that mining with nuclear explosives would be banned worldwide for these reasons alone.

Benefits. No benefits per se are estimated, because it is assumed that the benefit from equal amounts of produced copper are equal and comparisons are made for unit quantities of produced metal. The study could therefore be classified as a risk/risk analysis.

Uncertainties. The conclusions of the study and the summary table of estimates provided do not indicate the magnitude of the uncertainties involved (for the conventional method a range is given, but it is merely the range obtained by including or excluding the cost of air pollution "depending on population density and proximity"). The text indicates, however, that the range of uncertainties is very large, especially since the risks are assigned a dollar cost, a process that itself introduces large uncertainties.

The range of uncertainties is easiest to see in the estimation of the cost of environmental risks due to conventional mining. In the summary and conclusions these risks are given as follows:

- Sulfur oxides, $43/ton
- Water pollution, $7/ton (from use for flotation separation)
- Water pollution, $0.7/ton (from use for leaching)
- Pits, tailings, and dumps, $50/ton
- Accidental death and permanent disability, $21.75/ton
- Total $72–115/ton

Perusal of the text reveals that its author estimates an uncertainty of up to 5 to 1 in the figure for sulfur oxides and 4 to 1 for the pits, tailings, and dumps, while the cost of the environmental risk of water pollution is equated to the cost of temporary loss of water for other uses. Even with such a dubious definition, the cost of water for other uses varies by up to 40 to 1. Finally, the figure for accidental deaths and disabilities is uncertain, both statistically (the number of deaths varies year by year, and it is not clear that the figure given is an average) and through the procedure adopted for valuations of death or disability.

In the case of the nuclear method, all data must necessarily be uncertain, because no actual information exists, so that all is based on extrapolation. Many of the risks assessed depend on the population density within 50 miles or so of the plant. For the study it was assumed that there would be approximately 1,000 people resident within a radius of 50 miles, a population density of 0.13 persons per square mile. This should be contrasted with average (statewide) population densities of 4 per square mile (Wyoming) and higher (although Alaska has 0.7 persons per square mile on average, and the national average is ~ 61), which indicates that, unless a specific site is considered, the range of uncertainty here is very large. In this, as in other respects, no assessments or statements were made of these uncertainties.

The overall result of this lack of treatment is that little if any confidence can be placed on the final quoted figures or on comparisons between them, because the two figures are both uncertain by unknown and large amounts and because they are not comparable.

Aggregation. All risks are aggregated by assigning costs to them, and a benefit equal to the market value of the copper produced is assumed, resulting in a dimensionless benefit/risk ratio. Little meaning can be attached to these figures, however, because of the uncertainties and flaws mentioned.

Distribution of the Risks and Benefits. Although no explicit mention is made of the problem of distribution of the risks, it is partially treated implicitly in the text. Most risks considered are to people within 50 miles of the respective plants (all except air and water pollution), and the relative risks to such persons can be derived from the figures given (although these risks would be incomplete for the reasons explained earlier). The distribution of benefits is not considered, because this was supposed to be a comparison between two ways of obtaining the same benefit. Nevertheless, it is clear that there may be distributional problems (as in transport accidents involving conventional or nuclear explosives.)

Extensions

No extensions are easy; a major omitted risk—that of having many nuclear explosives in relatively common use—has worried many, but there is no agreement on how to begin to assess this risk.

CASE 6: MASS CHEST RADIOGRAPHY

- *Source*: Kitabatake, T.; M. Yokoyama; M. Sakka; and S. Koga. 1973. "Estimation of Benefit and Radiation Risk from Mass Chest Radiography." *Journal of Diagnostic Radiology* 109: 37–40.

- *Purpose*: Estimates of the benefits and the radiation risks of the mass chest X-ray survey in Japan in 1968.

- *Subject matter*: The mass chest X-ray survey performed in 1968, primarily as a screen for detection of tuberculosis.

- *Risks included*: Death from tuberculosis, leukemia, chest, and lung cancers and deaths from genetic effects induced by the radiation dose.

- *Costs included*: None.

- *Benefits included*: Diagnosis of disease and hence its treatment are the only benefits considered.

- *Alternatives considered*: None.

Summary of Methodology

Using data on the detection of tuberculosis from the mass chest fluorography campaign of 1968, in which 3.86×10^7 persons were examined, together with an estimated age distribution of the persons fluorographed, obtained in an independent survey, the age distribution of detected active pulmonary tuberculosis cases is estimated. Using the age-specific death rates for tuberculosis in Japan allows an estimate of the number of lethal cases among those detected, the remainder being assumed curable. Of the 44,447 detected cases, 38,629 are thus estimated as curable. In addition to tuberculosis, detection and cure of lung cancer are also considered, although much less detail is possible. Lung cancer detection rates based on relatively small populations are used to estimate a total detection of 3,024 cases of lung cancer, with a cure rate of perhaps 25 percent under the best conditions (the figures presented give a range of 3 to 25 percent). The benefit of the fluorography campaign is thus considered to be early diagnosis of 38,621 cases of curable active lung tuberculosis, and 758 curable cases of lung cancer. (Detection of nonactive tuberculous benign pulmonary disease is also reported, but the significance of such detection is not clear.)

Radiation risk from the mass fluorography campaign is computed separately for leukemia and other cancers, and also for genetic deaths, meaning deaths in future generations caused by radiation damage to germ cells in the gonads of the current generation. The leukemia significant dose is computed for each age group; the actual average bone marrow dose per exposure is thirty-five mrad for persons over fifteen, but the leukemia significant dose is lower by factors of one to three at ages less than fifteen and greater than seventy-five respectively. The expected incidence of leukemia is obtained by applying the incidence rate of 1.5 to 1.8 per 10^6 per rad per year observed in atom bomb survivors. This results in 1.82 leukemias per year, or about forty-six in twenty-five years. After whole-body irradiation, other cancers are expected to develop with about the same frequency as leukemias but with a longer latent period. Because only the chest is irradiated and chest cancers normally account for 15.5 percent of all lethal cancers, incurable chest cancers attributable to radiation are estimated at 15.5 percent of forty-six, which amounts to seven in twenty-five years.

Genetic deaths are assumed to be related to gonadal dose at the rate of $1.9 \times 10^3/10^6$/rad up to the tenth generation and $8.5 \times 10^3/10^6$/rad for all future generations. Since the gonads are not directly exposed during a chest X-ray, the dose to the gonads is small, and the authors estimate the total effects to be 150 deaths in ten generations and 670 for all future generations.

Conclusions of the Study

The conclusions are simply stated that the 3.86×10^7 X-rays of the chest performed in 1968 detected 44,447 cases of active tuberculosis, of which $\sim 38,600$ were curable, together with 758 curable lung cancer cases. The prevalence of tuberculosis in Japan has dropped from 3.2 percent in 1958 to 1.49 percent in 1968, with the mortality rate falling from 212 (in 10^5 per year) in 1940 to 16.8 in 1968, and it is widely accepted that mass chest fluorography has made a great contribution to this improvement. (For a population of 60 million, this reduction corresponds to a drop in annual deaths of $\sim 117,000$.) However, the effects of the 1968 fluorographies would be about forty-six leukemias and seven incurable chest cancers in the subsequent twenty-five years, with 150 genetic deaths in the next ten generations and 670 in all future generations.

Analysis

Objective. The limited objective of demonstrating the preponderance of benefit over risk for the particular mass X-ray campaign considered is apparently achieved. This may not be of much use in planning future campaigns, however, for there is evidently some level of tuberculosis incidence below which the expected benefit of reducing deaths from tuberculosis is outweighed by the excess deaths expected, because of the X-rays, in this and future generations, to say nothing of the economic cost of such campaigns. A more extensive and useful study might examine the possibility of some form of selective screening to some fraction of the population prior to X-ray exposure, compare the risks and costs of alternative methods of detection of tuberculosis, and investigate whether the same results could be achieved with lower X-ray exposures (the 1968 exposure of 35 mrad to 3.86×10^7 persons is a total population dose equal to approximately 10 percent of the natural background in that year, although the X-ray exposure was only to the chest).

Assumptions. As acknowledged by the authors, there are a number of unstated assumptions that bias the evaluation of benefits and risks, although since the authors leave the readers to their own conclusions (see "Aggregation of Risks and Benefits" below) the effects of the bias are unclear. It is assumed that the number of curable active tuberculosis cases may be found as the difference between those detected and the expected lethal number in the fluorographed population. The assumption ignores the possibility of remission among untreated cases and thus may possibly overstate any benefit of detection. The number of curable lung cancer cases is likewise an upper bound even when based on the figures for success of treatment given in the article. Estimation of likely direct radiation induced diseases is based on the data from atomic bomb survivors and is not likely to overestimate these effects, even though no credit is allowed for the possibility of cure in some cases.

Risks. The major risks to the population of the fluorography campaign are treated. No estimate is made of any occupational risk to those manning the X-ray machines. The integrated dose to the X-ray technicians is clearly less than that to the patients and the societal risk is less, but the risk to an individual may be high and therefore important.

Benefits and Costs. No attempt is made to estimate the costs of the campaign, although such estimates are probably readily available. Similarly, no attempt is made to estimate the benefits, say in the form of reduction in man-days lost, resulting from early diagnosis.

Uncertainties. One failing of the paper is that it does not indicate the large uncertainties in all the estimates made. Indeed, the figures are given an unreal precision by being quoted with up to five significant figures. Just as there are uncertainties about benefits, there are similar large uncertainties in the risks due to radiation dose. Although these uncertainties may be large, they are unlikely to result in more lives lost through radiation deaths than lives saved through detection of tuberculosis, at least in this particular case. It does not follow, of course, that the same would be true in a different population, so the result is specific to the particular campaign of fluorography studied, as is underscored by the authors in encouraging risk/benefit studies for future campaigns.

Aggregation of Risks, Benefits, and Costs. All risks and benefits are measured by the numbers of deaths caused or averted, so they may easily be compared. This simplicity of comparison is only an illusion; not only are certain risks and benefits neglected, but also the uncertainties.

Distribution of Risks, Benefits, and Costs. Societal risks only are considered in this paper. In practice, the only benefit, apart from peace of mind, accrues to those diagnosed as having tuberculosis (or lung cancer) whereas the risks are spread over the whole population X-rayed (or the whole population, for genetic effects), as presumably are the costs, assuming the campaign was a public health measure provided free of direct charge. Such distribution is unavoidable in any screening program but deserves mention because such risks, even though miniscule, may be taken voluntarily but rejected when involuntary.

Extensions

Although "it is widely accepted that mass chest fluorography has made a great contribution to tuberculosis prevention in Japan" (p. 40), and the study shows a vast preponderance of deaths averted, it does not follow that this is the last word. A more extensive study might examine the effects of selective screening prior to X-ray exposure or compare costs and risks of alternative methods of tuberculosis detection. Similarly, some effort is required to decide whether the same diagnostic efficiency could be achieved with less X-ray exposure, possibly at greater expense. Last, any risk/cost/benefit analysis will be affected by the incidence rate of tuberculosis in the population examined, so that for certain portions of the population, if the incidence is low enough, risk may outweigh benefits. This is likely to occur as tuberculosis is wiped out, so that any decisions about mass radiography should have an automatic review period.

CASE 7: SKULL FRACTURE DIAGNOSIS

- *Source*: Bell, R.S. and J.W. Loop. 1971. "The Utility and Futility of Radiographic Skull Examination for Trauma." *The New England Journal of Medicine* 284: 236–239.
- *Original context*: A four-page special article.
- *Purpose*: "[f]irst an attempt to discover the current information yield of skull series [of X-rays] taken for [head] injury and secondly an investigation to determine if there is some rational strategy for selecting skull radiographs."
- *Subject matter*: Radiographic, or X-ray, examination of the skull is considered as a technique that, through the additional information it supplies, may improve the prognosis for cases of trauma to the head. An attempt is made to assess its efficacy for this purpose, and to search for any indicators of those cases in which it may be omitted.
- *Risks included*: The only risk evaluated is that of possible misdiagnosis leading to inappropriate treatment of the patients, both with and without the adoption of the scheme proposed by the authors. The risk of cancer from use of X-rays is omitted.

- *Costs included*: No extra costs are mentioned.

- *Benefits included*: The estimated monetary benefits of the scheme proposed are given, based simply on the reduction of the number of radiographic examinations that would be required.

Summary of Methodology

Questionnaires supplied to two large medical centers were completed prospectively for all cases referred for skull X-ray examinations. Approximately 90 percent of the skull examinations in these two medical centers in a thirteen-month period were covered, and all cases of skull fractures found in the remaining 10 percent were retrospectively included. The questionnaires required the physician requesting the X-rays to detail clinical findings, his or her estimate of the likelihood of fracture, and reasons for the request; the X-rays were subsequently evaluated by radiologists. The authors discuss the various biases resulting from this procedure and from the existence of the questionnaire and estimate that any conclusions would overstate the utility of the X-ray series. In 1,500 skull series, ninety-three fractures were found, excluding old fractures. Correlations between the presence of a fracture and items on the questionnaires giving clinical history and physical examination results identified a set of twenty-one high-yield items, although in the event of any one such item most patients did not have a fracture, and no single item was present in a majority of the patients with fractures. It was also found that the physician's estimate was relatively accurate, the yield of fractures increasing with the physician's estimate of severity, but that the likelihood of fracture was overestimated. Twenty-eight of the ninety-three patients found to have fractures had their treatment altered because of this demonstration, although the alterations were in the form of prophylactic measures to prevent low-probability complications.

As a possible patient selection strategy, the authors suggest the use of their twenty-one findings as a screen, requiring the presence of at least one of those findings as a necessary condition for X-ray treatment. In retrospect, only one of the ninety-three patients with a fracture would not have had radiographs taken, and that patient's treatment was not altered by the radiographic confirmation of a fracture, while 434 (29 percent of the total number) of the patients without fractures would have been X-rayed. Since 20–30 percent of the 8×10^6 head and neck X-ray examinations taken each year, at a cost of $50–60 \times 10^6$, in the United States are to evaluate head injury, the strategy could give savings of "$15–20 \times 10^6$."

Conclusions of the Study

Although no definite conclusion is ever stated, it is strongly implied that automatic X-ray examinations for skull fractures are inappropriate and that the use of the twenty-one case history items as a screen, requiring at least one such item to be present before ordering skull series X-rays for suspected fractures, would be an appropriate policy to be adopted nationally. The estimated savings would be 15×10^6 per year nationally, assuming the authors' results to be representative.

Analysis

Objectives. It is clearly demonstrated that a lot of information was yielded by the skull series X-rays in this study, but it mainly disproved a faint possibility of skull fracture—50 percent of the X-rays were performed with an estimation of only a one in 100 chance of any finding, with a true rate of only one in 378, and 34 percent were performed for purely medicolegal reasons. The utility of X-rays in these cases was thus very low. The second objective of finding a rational strategy is fulfilled by the presentation of a preliminary "screen" of twenty-one findings in a case history, which, taken together, would have given reasonable reduction in numbers of X-rays required with only a slight chance of failure to detect a fracture, at least in the set of patients observed. Whether this strategy would work equally well on another group of patients requires further testing, of course, but it is a good start. In view of the monetary savings that would accrue and the unevaluated reduction in cancer risk, attempts to confirm the efficacy of the screening method appear to be worthwhile, although it is possible that a need to protect the physician against malpractice suits will lead physicans to order X-rays until this screening procedure is well established.

Assumptions. It is implicitly assumed throughout the article that discovery of a skull fracture would be beneficial for the patient (even though 34 percent of the examinations were requested primarily for medicolegal reasons—for the benefit of the doctor, to protect against legal suits). In fact, of the ninety-three patients with fractures actually discovered, twenty-eight had their courses of therapy altered because of the discovery, and even then the alteration was the application of prophylactic measures, the risks of which were not discussed, measures designed to counter possible complications, ones that "develop in a minority of even untreated patients." Apart from this, other assumptions are clearly stated.

Risks. The only effective measure of risk included in the study is that of misdiagnosis. No numerical estimate is made of any possible consequence of misdiagnosis, either with or without the screening method proposed by the authors. No mention is made of the slight additional risks arising from the use of X-rays, although this should be small, or of the possible risks of prophylactic therapy in the cases where skull fracture is confirmed. The prophylactic therapies mentioned are antibiotic treatment and surgical operations for depressed fractures, used in attempts to prevent meningitis and epilepsy, both of which treatments have nonzero risks, the former from possible adverse reactions to the chosen antibiotics, the latter from adverse reactions to anaesthetics and the possibility of infection.

Benefits and Costs. Although the benefits of discovery of skull fractures are not discussed, the yearly total cost of X-ray examinations of head and neck for evaluation of head injury is put at $50–60 \times 10^6$ in the United States (for 1967) with an individual skull series costing \$30. Thus the authors' suggested screening procedure would reduce the annual cost by $15–20 \times 10^6$ (extrapolating to the entire United States). No estimate is made of any additional cost of their procedure, but it would presumably be comparatively small.

Uncertainties. Numerical estimates of risks are not given, so neither are their uncertainties. Conclusions about cost are drawn about the entire United States from a sample of 1,500 patients, which should give reasonably reliable predictions for the $1.6–2.4 \times 10^6$ examinations per year actually undertaken for head injury evaluation, provided the sample is not biased. There is no discussion of any such possible biases.

Aggregation of Risks and Benefits.   Some minor attempt is made to aggregate risks and benefits, but it is incomplete. The survey predicts a cost of $7,650 to find each fracture (at $30 per skull series) in the medicolegal group, examinations done purely for medicolegal purposes, and $11,340 per fracture in the "one-in-hundred-chance" group. Both these estimates are subject to large uncertainty, since only two fractures in each group were found, out of, respectively, 757 and 509 total examinations. Note also that the two groups are not mutually exclusive. If only 30 percent of the fractures are serious, in the sense that their discovery alters therapy, the cost per serious fracture in each case rises to $25,500 and $37,800, respectively. The authors make no judgment as to whether these costs are excessive but point out that at some level the cost does become prohibitive. Completeness would require an evaluation of the risks and other benefits or costs mentioned previously and some attempt at comparing these. The authors do not complete their proposed alternative procedure by an evaluation of the risks, costs, and benefits in a differential comparison along the same lines.

Distribution of Risks and Benefits.   No mention is made of the distribution of the risks, benefits, and costs. But it is probable that most benefit accrues to those patients in which skull fractures are discovered. The costs are shared by all the patients undergoing X-ray examination or by a large segment of society through medical insurance. Similarly risks from X-ray examinations are incurred by all patients, with a small component also to the operating staff.

CASE 8: CORONARY ARTERY SURGERY

- *Source*:   Pauker, S.G. 1976. "Coronary Artery Surgery: The Use of Decision Analysis." *Annals of Internal Medicine*, 85: 8–18.

- *Purpose*:   The article attempts to detail how a formal decision analysis can be used as an aid to the physician in the decision on the treatment to be applied in individual cases of chronic ischemic heart disease, taking into account the patients' preferences.

- *Subject matter*: In each case of coronary artery disease, the physician has to decide between coronary by-pass surgery and conservative medical therapy. Each treatment varies in its attendant risks, depending on the features present in the disease in the individual. Moreover, each patient has his or her own outlook regarding the severity of the risks. For example, some people may prefer five years of pain-filled life on one treatment regime to the possibility of immediate death in an alternative treatment designed to relieve them of the pain. The paper attempts to take into account three main variables that determine the value of coronary by-pass surgery: the outcome of the surgery, the outcome of alternative treatment, and the preferences of the patient. The outcome of either surgery or alternative treatment depends on the severity of the disease, classified into four groups for the purpose of the study. Outcome of surgery also depends on the skill of the operating team, which was classified as "excellent," "good," or "average." Patient preference was classified into four groups depending on their relative valuation of pain and length of life.

- *Risks included*: The risks evaluated are the changes in expectation of life due to the two alternative treatment regimes, including the possibility of immediate death in the case of by-pass surgery and the possibility of change in level of pain experienced by the patient.

- *Costs included*: No costs are discussed in the analysis, and no estimates are made of any possible costs of using the analysis method outlined.

- *Benefits included*: No monetary benefits are included in the analysis, except insofar as they would enter patient preferences to some extent. Any possible benefits of actually applying the analysis method are not evaluated.

Summary of Methodology

The first step of the method is the construction of a "decision tree" starting at the surgery/no surgery decision and continuing through various branches to describe all possible outcomes. For simplicity, "quality of life" is limited to one of two states, "pain" and "no pain." The resultant decision tree is shown in Figure 6–2 up to the time immediately following surgery.

Figure 6-2. First Part of the Decision Tree for Coronary Artery Surgery.

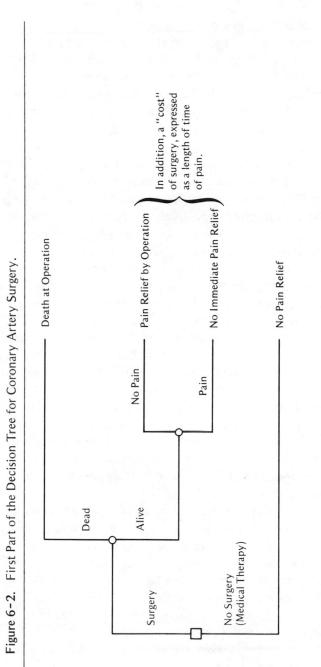

Subsequent branches of the tree consider the possibilities of heart attacks in the subsequent five years, each heart attack possibly killing the patient or changing the pain status. The final number of outcomes can be large, but each can be labeled by a length of time alive and length of time with and without pain. Once the tree is constructed, the probabilities of all the outcomes may be simply computed if the probabilities for each branch point are known. Data are presented giving details of the probabilities (as a function of disease severity and skill of the operating team, classified on the basis of past results) for each branch point, evaluated from published studies or from estimates made by experienced cardiologists. As the author notes, these evaluations are likely to have been made on small and selected groups, so the values have large associated uncertainties, but this is dealt with by using a sensitivity analysis.

Probabilities of the outcomes having been obtained, values have to be assigned to the outcomes, consonant with their value to the individual patient. It is assumed that to each patient there corresponds a utility function based on the form, Utility = $z(1 - \exp(-k\,t))$, where z is an arbitrary scale factor, t is the time free of pain or length of life, and k is a positive constant describing the patient's risk aversion, larger values of k describing more risk-averse persons. For the purpose of this trial study, patients are divided into four types: (1) those concerned mainly with time free of pain (the group labeled "pain"), (2) those concerned primarily with length of life (type "life"), (3) those to whom either freedom from pain or life expectancy were important (type "either"), and (4) those to whom both were of such importance that pain relief was not acceptable unless life expectancy increased also (type "both").

Type pain patients are assigned a utility function with $k = 1$ (time measured in years) corresponding to utility increasing almost linearly with time free of pain. Life patients (more risk averse) are assigned $k = 3$, corresponding to rapid initial increase in utility with lifetime. Both utility functions are scaled to give utility = 100 after five years of time free of pain or five years of life. Utility curves for type either patients are obtained by averaging the utilities arithmetically for the same outcome of the first two types, while for type both patients the geometric mean is used, because only if both utilities are large is the geometric mean large.

Although the article uses these utility curves for its examples, it points out that in any individual case it is possible to debrief individual patients to obtain their own individual utility functions (a short summary of the method is given), so that the procedure may be individually tailored. Using the patients' utility functions allows the utility of each outcome to be computed.

The relative worth of surgical and medical therapy may then be evaluated by multiplying the utility of each possible outcome of either therapy (that is, for surgery, all the outcomes connected back on the decision tree to the first surgery branch, and similarly for no surgery–medical therapy) by that outcome's probability of occurrence, to obtain the expected value of the utility for the two possibilities. Decision theory then states that one should prefer the therapy with the larger expected value, and the difference between these expected values measures to some degree the extent of the preference.

Conclusions of the Study

The author applies the method to the four hypothetical patient types described for four categories of illness severity and with three levels of surgical skill (a total of forty-eight analyses). In general it is found that surgery was preferable for patients of type "pain," "either," or "both," and medical therapy preferable for type "life" patients, if their illness was such that they suffered severe pain (disabling angina). For asymptomatic patients, medical therapy was preferred except in one case. A sensitivity analysis indicated that the choice of therapy would be little affected by small changes in the input data (probabilities at branch points in the decision tree). Similarly having little effect were changes in the model such as extension of the time horizon, the cost of surgery expressed as the equivalent time in pain, and the number of heart attacks considered—and thus the size of the decision tree. It is shown that a model with only ten outcomes (only one heart attack considered) gave results similar to one with 190 outcomes (five heart attacks), so that a physician could calculate just a ten-branch tree for an individual patient.

Analysis

Objective. Although the article succeeds admirably in its primary task of informing an individual physican of a method he or she may use to aid in the choice of therapy for an individual patient and gives a good indication of the probable results of such application of the method under various conditions, it is clear that any physician faced with the task of applying it in an individual case would confront major problems. For although the physician could use many of the data presented in the paper, some would require replacement with location-specific values, that is, probabilities assigned to various outcomes of surgery, which might be difficult to obtain, and others with patient-specific values, the patient's utility function, which would be time consuming to obtain. Although the article includes three illustrative cases of individual patients it is not clear whether two of them were actually debriefed to obtain "assumed" utilities for the various outcomes.

Assumptions.   Most assumptions of the method are explicitly stated, and it is demonstrated that sensitivity analysis may be used to test the effects of variation of at least some of them. In discussing the application to an individual patient, it is implicitly assumed that the patient's orally expressed preferences are in fact his or her preferences, a point that requires analysis.

Risks.   The risks considered are those of the patient's immediate death, change in life expectation, and change in pain following surgery. The probabilities of such events under various conditions had to be included in the analysis. None of these probabilities is known accurately; indeed some of those used were simply best estimates of experienced cardiologists. Nevertheless, the sensitivity analyses show that the results of applying the method are insensitive to the precise values used, so that this is not a major shortcoming.

Costs and Benefits.   No monetary costs are considered in any of the discussion, although it is clear that the costs of applying the analysis suggested would not be substantial, perhaps equivalent to an hour or two of time. The benefits arising from its use would be intangible—a possible increase in the patient's utility through the correct choice of therapy, possibly greater physician awareness of individual patient's feelings—although such benefits are not discussed. Perhaps the main benefit would accrue to the physican in being provided with a clear framework for ordering of a logical pattern of thought, taking into account likely outcomes and patient preferences.

Besides costs and benefits to the individual patient, there are possible costs and benefits to society. Any method that increases the likelihood of taking a "correct" course of action, one that increases an individual's utility, increases the utility of society as a whole if widely applied, and presumably this is beneficial. On the other hand, in the absence of data on the costs of these treatments or the actual change in treatment pattern, it is not possible to estimate any net monetary costs to society.

Uncertainties. Uncertainties in the method presented are dealt with by application of sensitivity analyses, which indicate how uncertain the decision is within the model framework. Most uncertainty in any such decision comes from factors not included in the model, so that it is up to the physician to attempt to account for these on a case-by-case basis.

Aggregation of Risks, Costs, and Benefits. The idea behind the method suggested is aggregation of risks with the at least partly intangible benefits to the patient as measured by his or her utility function. Costs are not considered at all except insofar as different costs of different therapies if known to the patient may affect the patient's utility function. It might be possible to explicitly include in a similar methodology any costs of treatment borne by the patient by finding the effects of cost on his or her utility function. For example, it is possible that one may prefer a chance of immediate death followed by freedom from pain to continued pain but prefer the pain to being a pauper free of pain.

Distribution of Risks, Costs, and Benefits. The risks and benefits are all considered as accruing to the individual patient. As mentioned previously, no attempt is made to consider a broader context.

CASE 9: SWINE INFLUENZA IMMUNIZATION

- *Source:* Schoenbaum, S.C.; B.J. McNeil; and J. Kavet. 1976. "The Swine Influenza Decision," *The New England Journal of Medicine*, 295: 759–765.

- *Purpose:* "To demonstrate the feasibility of analysing formally the influenza vaccine decision within the time constraints posed by the actual situation."

- *Subject matter*: A formal and quantitative method of decision making to include subjective estimates of the probabilities of the various risks, costs, and benefits associated with various vaccination programs, and a retrospective use of that method for the case of the swine influenza decision.

- *Risks included*: Complications and death from influenza and complications from vaccination.

- *Costs included*: Direct costs for physicians' services, hospital services, and prescription drugs. Indirect costs of lost productivity due to temporary incapacitation or death for both influenza and vaccination. Costs of vaccine production and administration.

- *Benefits included*: Defined as costs avoided by the vaccination program—the product of the costs that would be incurred in the event of an epidemic, the probability of an epidemic, and the vaccine's efficacy. Also calculated are numbers of cases averted and years of life saved by the vaccination programs considered.

Summary of Methodology

An estimate is made of the direct and indirect costs of an influenza epidemic. The direct costs are computed from data on physician attendance on victims (41.7 percent according to the National Health Survey), hospitalization rate (3 percent of victims) estimated by age, length of stay estimated by age (by analogy with pneumonia, the range is six to twelve days), and financial charges from Massachusetts and national data ($10.40 per office visit, $4.25 per patient attended for prescription charges, $139.50 per day hospital cost, in-hospital physician charges of $31.20 on admission and $10.40 per day). Indirect costs are the value of productivity lost (using 1975 estimated daily earnings and an average work loss of 2.8 days per episode, from national data), and losses due to premature death, assumed to be equal to estimates of the present value of lifetime earnings discounted at 4, 6, or 8 percent. In these estimates the presence of high-risk groups and the possibility of more than one influenza attack are taken into account.

The cost of various vaccination programs is estimated, with the vaccine assumed to cost in large quantities about $0.50 per dose. Three programs, involving vaccination of the general population over four years of age, the general population over twenty-four years of age, or just the high-risk population, with total vaccine cost being $100 million, $60 million, and $24 million, respectively, are analyzed with two possible delivery systems. The first, the variable cost system, assumes the use of private physicians, with administration cost per person vaccinated at $2.27. The second, the fixed cost system, is based on the use of public clinics, with an administration cost dependent only on the size of the target group, not on the response by the target group. Here the cost is estimated at $0.50 per person in the target group, giving an administration cost equal to the cost of vaccine for the whole target group. The cost of reactions to the vaccine is estimated by assuming one day's loss of work per serious reaction.

Important variables in the decision on a vaccination program that are not amenable to statistical treatment are the possibility of an epidemic, age-specific morbidity and mortality for the general and the high-risk population, vaccine efficacy, vaccine reaction rate, and acceptance rates in the target population. All these variables were obtained by a Delphi survey. Initially five experts in influenza epidemiology and subsequently ten experts with a broader range of expertise were asked their professional opinion on these subjects.

Using the data gathered, the net benefits in monetary terms are calculated. A sensitivity analysis is then performed to determine the effects of variations in the estimates of epidemic probability, acceptance rates for the program (the number of people in the program who accept the vaccine), vaccine efficacies, and discount rates.

In addition, the expected number of influenza cases averted and the expected number of years of life saved are calculated using the same variables together with standard life tables. Results are presented in the form of graphs, one for each program, showing the net benefits as a function of acceptance rate, together with the variation caused by variation of discount rate.

Conclusions of the Study

Essentially two types of conclusions are drawn by the authors of this study, first, from the analysis itself and, second from the time it took to perform the analysis. The analysis indicates that if vaccination is given entirely in private practice the program would break even only if it were aimed at the high-risk group, and even then the net benefits are less than for the same program administered publicly. For the publicly administered programs, the expected net benefits are not maximized by immunization of the entire population five years old and older. Immunization of large segments of the population, say twenty-five years and older, can be justified only if certain conditions are fulfilled; the conditions include high efficacy for the vaccine, low costs for its administration, and high acceptance rates, together with the assumption that the influenza is a new, potentially pandemic strain. If the conditions are not fulfilled, a program aimed only at the high-risk group yields the greatest net benefits. The authors point out that they have assessed only economic benefits. The noneconomic costs per case averted—discomfort or death—vary markedly and nonlinearly with the acceptance rates, and furthermore the lowest costs per case averted, but the highest cost per year of life saved, occur in the general population program whereas the opposite, the highest cost per case averted, lowest per year of life saved, occurs in programs limited to the high-risk group.

The second type of conclusion drawn from this analysis comes from the time required to conduct it, four weeks. Because this much time is usually available for such a decision, it appears feasible to conduct such an analysis to assist in the decision making. The formal analysis performed indicates the parameters of importance, and the Delphi technique ensures the best expert opinion of the values and ranges of the parameters. This contrasts with the usual practice of convening groups of experts and requesting specific recommendations on policy.

Comments

The analysis is complete and informative and convincingly demonstrates the benefits of using such a formal tool in policy formulation. In particular, it shows clearly how the greatest economic benefit to the nation could be obtained and how the program to obtain this might conflict with the desire of the individual to avoid the noneconomic cost of suffering from influenza.

Although it is possible to argue that some of the costs used in the analysis are incorrect measures of actual costs (for example, lifetime discounted earning for the effective cost of a life), sensitivity analyses within the formal framework permit the evaluation of the effect of this. Similarly, although intangibles such as pain or suffering are excluded, they are highlighted as noted previously and could be included, at least crudely, if analysts were prepared to assign some sort of cost to them.

An extension of the analysis might include the possibility of modifying a program as actual data became available on vaccine efficacy, epidemic likelihood, and public acceptance of that program. Nevertheless it is clear that even in its present form, an analysis such as this would have been of great assistance in making the decision and may have resulted in an alternative vaccination program. A well-argued and well-documented analysis can also lead to public confidence and support for the decision, a nonnegligible political advantage for such a process.

REFERENCES

American Council on Science and Health. 1979. *Saccharin.* New York, New York.

Cohen, B.L. 1978. "Saccharin: The Risks and Benefits." *Nature* 271: 492.

Kemeny, J.G. (Chairman) et al. 1979. *The Need for Change: The Legacy of TMI.* Report of the President's Commission on the Accident at Three Mile Island. Washington, D.C.: U.S. Government Printing Office.

Lave, L., and E. Seskin. 1970. "Air Pollution and Human Health." *Science* 169: 723.

Lewis, H.A. (Chairman) et al. 1978. "Risk Assessment Review Group Report to the U.S. Nuclear Regulatory Commission." NUREG/CR-0400. Washington, D.C.

National Academy of Sciences. 1972. *The Effects on Populations of Exposure to Low Levels of Ionizing Radiations.* Report of the Advisory Committee on the Biological Effects of Ionizing Radiations (BEIR 1). Washington, D.C.

7 EVERYDAY LIFE
A Catalogue of Risks

It is unquestionably true that it [rail travel] is safer than travelling by coach or on horseback . . . if one wants anything safer he must walk.

> H.G. Prout. 1892. *The American Railway*
> New York: Charles Scribner and Son, p. 191.

This book opened with the statement that life is a risky business. What this meant was explained in qualitative terms, and then ways of quantitatively estimating the magnitudes of various measures of risk were described. The knowledge of risk magnitudes is of little use, however, unless they can be related to the magnitudes of everyday risks, for otherwise no sense is given of the importance of the risks and how much notice should be taken of them.

This chapter is devoted to showing just how (quantitatively) risky is everyday life by assigning numerical values to a collection of common actions that involve some element of risk. The object is to provide a background of values for familiar risks, against which the results of calculations of unfamiliar risks may be judged. Throughout the chapter we shall be discussing risks of death, so that the risk measure used will be the probability of death, sometimes a population-weighted average annual probability, at other times age-specific annual average probabilities, and occasionally other averages. We do not claim to present a complete list of risks.

165

In order to present all the risks on as common a basis as possible, we have tried to arrange our examples so that we can specify some quantity or measure of activity that will give either a lifetime probability of 10^{-6} (one in a million) of dying from that activity or an annual probability of 10^{-6} of dying. The average lifetime in the United States is about seventy-two years; hence for any given risk there will be a factor 72 difference between the numerical values of such measures, provided that any annual probabilities given are averaged over all ages according to the age structure of the population and provided the risks are small enough.

THE RISK OF LIVING

The first risk (of death) to consider is that in living itself—that is, the probability of dying. If this sounds paradoxical, it must be noted that the sum of all lifetime average risks (of death) must be 1 (absolute certainty), because everybody dies. From the risk analyst's point of view, it might be said that the object of living is to die! Society's efforts go into attempting to reduce annual risks, in order to make it more likely that the inevitable death will occur later, so that longevity is increased.

We look first at the probability of dying because it corresponds to the sum of all the risks to which people are exposed. If we had a complete list of all activities undertaken by everybody, together with a list of the risks involved in such activities, and provided that we took care to avoid double counting, we could add all the risks together to obtain the total risk of dying. Evidently, for any individual or group, such a sum would vary from individual to individual or group to group, but if we average everything over the whole population we simply get the average risk of dying for that population.

Figures 7–1 and 7–2 show the time required to accumulate a probability of 1 in 10^6 of dying at a given age for the population of the United States in 1974. This is a measure of the reciprocal of the total risk of living. Notice the changes of scale in Figure 7–1 and the logarithmic scale in Figure 7–2. The long range of times is better shown on the logarithmic scale of Figure 7–2, but Figure 7–1 may show this more dramatically for readers unfamiliar with logarithmic plots.

Figure 7-1. Time Required to Accumulate in Probability of 1 in 10^6 of Dying.

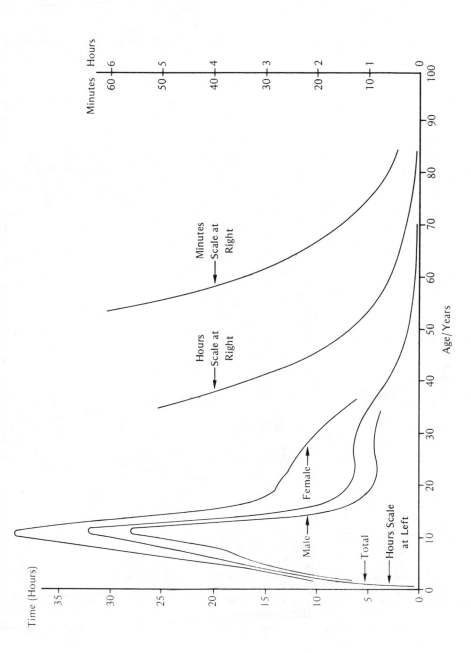

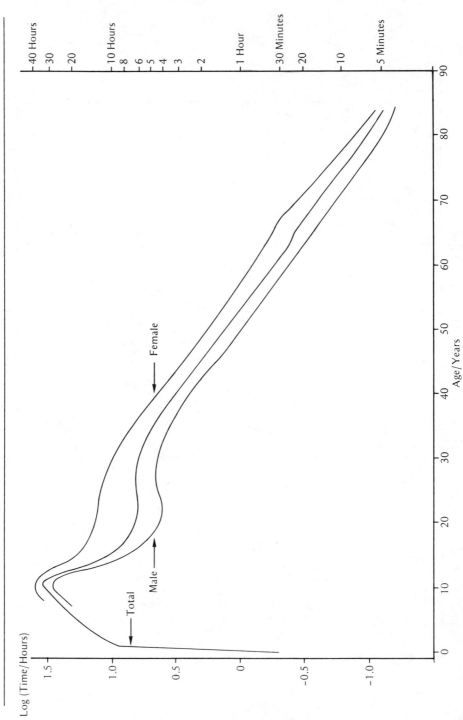

Figure 7–2. Logarithm of Time (in Hours) in Which Probability of Dying Is 1 in 10^6, versus Age.

As can be seen, the time required increases rapidly with age initially, reaching a maximum of twenty-eight to thirty-nine hours at age ten to eleven, and then falls rapidly. The dip in the curves near age twenty-one to twenty-two, especially pronounced in males, is caused mainly by the risks of automobile accidents. After age thirty the curves decrease steadily (this is especially obvious on Figure 7-2), reaching five to seven minutes at age eighty. These curves are, of course, just the reciprocal of the age-specific death rate curves for the United States' population and convey the same information. If we know the number N of males aged twenty, for example, in the population, and the time to accumulate 1 in 10^6 probability of dying for males aged twenty is 4.4 hours (from Figure 7-1), then in one year the probability of death is $(8,760/4.4) \times 10^{-6} = 1.2 \times 10^{-3}$, and so 1.2×10^{-3} N males aged twenty die each year.

Life Expectancies

Figure 7-1 and 7-2 correspond to what occurred in the United States in 1974. From year to year the probabilities of dying change gradually as changes occur in our society, so they are not strictly applicable to other years, although the rate of change is small. Assuming that these probabilities remain constant, it is possible to calculate what the population age structure (represented, for example, by the fraction surviving to a given age) would be if the same number of children were born each year and all grew up subject to the age-specific risks of Figures 7-1 and 7-2. The result is shown in Figure 7-3, where it is seen that most people would survive until their sixties, but there is a rapid drop off in survivors after seventy. The average age of the population shown in Figure 7-3 is known as the expectation of life at birth in 1974. It is the expected length of life of a child born in 1974. In actual fact, of course, such a child faces different risks; the actual risk for that child at age five is the five-year-old's risk in 1979, not in 1974.

Life expectancy at birth is thus an average measure of the risk of dying at all ages, the risks at all ages being taken into account in computing it, and is thus a measure that may be used to compare different dates to see if risks have been increasing or decreasing on average. The variation of expectation of life (at birth) with date is shown for the United States in Figure 7-4. As can be seen, the expectation of

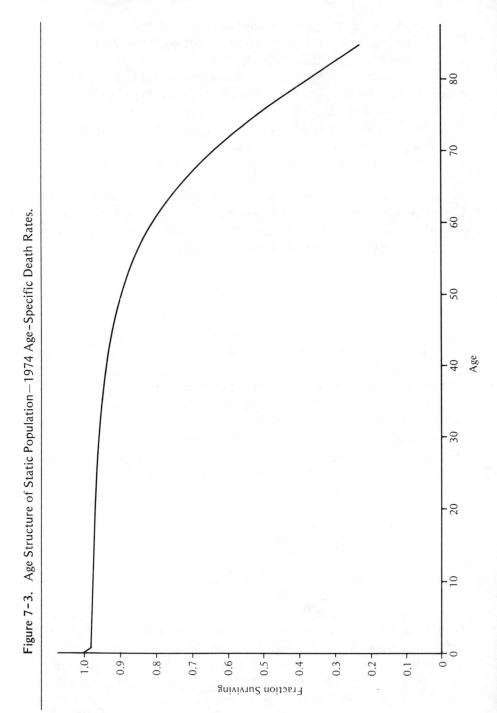

Figure 7-3. Age Structure of Static Population — 1974 Age-Specific Death Rates.

Figure 7-4. Expectation of Life at Birth in the United States, 1900–77.

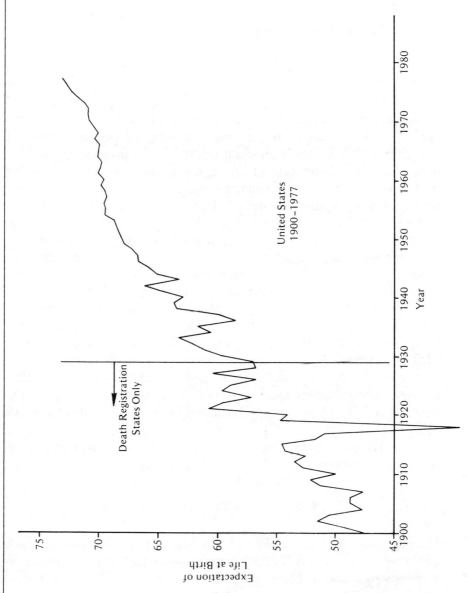

life has been increasing steadily, corresponding to a steady decline in the average annual risk of death.

Loss of Life Expectancy

In a similar way to that used to derive the expectation of life at birth, one can evaluate the expectation of life at any given age—the expected time to death of a person of that given age and subjected in the future to the age-specific risks a particular year, in our example 1974. Any changes in the risks to which any person is exposed will change that person's expectation of life, an increase in the risks decreasing the expectation of life, and a decrease in risks increasing it. The magnitude of such changes—the loss of life expectancy—can be computed by using tables of death rates. Schwing (1979) and Preston et al. (1972) give further details.

Although such methods must be used to obtain precise results, for our purposes it is straightforward to make a reasonably accurate estimate of the loss of life expectancy due to any given risk. Figure 7-3 shows that most people would survive to the sixties if they faced current age-specific risks, but few would survive past the early eighties. So we may approximate Figure 7-3 by a curve in which all survive to age seventy-two, the expectation of life at birth, and then all die. Then an excess risk p at age t leads to a loss of life expectancy of just $(72 - t) \times p$ years, and with averaging over the population (that is, over all ages) an excess risk p leads to an average loss of life expectancy of $36\,p$ years, or approximately nineteen minutes for a risk of 10^{-6}.

If the risk is a continuing one, say p per year, the loss of life expectancy is just

$$\sum_{t=0}^{72} (72 - t) \times p \approx 72 \times 36\,p \approx 2{,}600\,p \ ,$$

because there is a probability p of a loss of $(72 - t)$ years for each of the ages t from 0 to 72. An excess risk of 10^{-6} per year thus corresponds to a loss of life expectancy of $2{,}600 \times 10^{-6}$ year = 1 day, which is just 72 times the loss calculated in the previous paragraph.

The same approach may be taken if the risk is not constant throughout the lifetime, using actual annual risk probabilities, to yield approximate results (although it is not difficult to use the exact methods. Accidents, for example, lead to an average loss of life expectancy of about thirty years, whereas concers, diseases primarily of old age, results in an average loss of fourteen years.

The concept of risk needs a little care in definition when the deleterious effect is delayed from the cause. In our illustrative tables both cause and effect are averaged over all ages of occurrence. Averaging can be illustrated by the example of cigarette smoking, which most people now recognize as deleterious to health.

The U.S. surgeon general (Department of Health, Education, and Welfare 1979) estimates that 350,000 people will die annually from cigarette smoking. By dividing by an average annual number of cigarettes smoked (~ 650 billion), we find a risk of 0.5×10^{-6} per cigarette. Cancers reduce life expectancy by about eighteen years, so this risk corresponds to a reduction of about ten minutes per cigarette smoked (about the same time as it takes to smoke the cigarette!). Note that by using annual numbers dying and annual cigarette consumption, we have automatically averaged over all ages in the population, both for smoking of cigarettes and for dying of cancer induced by such smoking, even though the smoking precedes the cancer by many years. (This is an underestimate of the loss of life expectancy, though not of risk of death, because many of the deaths are due to heart disease and other ailments occurring earlier in life.)

A SELECTION OF RISKS

We have now provided background by showing how long in normal life it takes to accumulate a risk of 1 in 10^6 (one in a million) of dying, depending on age, and given another yardstick to judge a risk of 1 in 10^6, that it corresponds to a loss of life expectancy of nineteen minutes on average, while a person exposed to a risk of 1 in 10^6 for each year of life has life expectancy reduced by one day. In Table 7–1 we list some of the risks that everyone faces, posed in a form such that each corresponds to a risk of 1 in 10^6. The table should help to place different risks in perspective, but because some of the interpretations have to be strained a little to fit the format, they are difficult to compare.

Because it is often desirable to compare risks of the same type if possible; we present four more lists where risks are grouped more

Table 7-1. Some One in a Million Risks.

Living in the United States: Time to accumulate a one in a million risk of death from the cause indicated.

Motor vehicle accident	1.5 days
Falls	6 days
Drowning	10 days
Fires	13 days
Firearms	36 days
Electrocution	2 months
Tornadoes	20 months
Floods	20 months
Lightning	2 years
Animal bite or sting	4 years

Occupational Risks. Time to accumulate a one in a million risk of death in the occupation indicated.

General

Manufacturing	4.5 days
Trade	7 days
Service and Government	3.5 days
Transport and Public Utilities	1 day
Agriculture	15 hours
Construction	14 hours
Mining and Quarrying	9 hours

Specific

Coal Mining (accidents)	14 hours
Police duty	1.5 days
Railroad Employment	1.5 days
Fire Fighting	11 hours

Other Risks.

Cosmic Rays.

One transcontinental round trip by air.
Living 1.5 months in Colorado compared to New York.
Camping at 15,000 feet for 6 days compared to sea level.

Other Radiation

20 days of sea level natural background radiation.
2.5 months in masonry rather than wood building.
1/7 of a chest X-ray using modern equipment.

Table 7-1. continued

Eating and Drinking.
 40 diet sodas (saccharin)
 6 pounds of peanut butter (aflatoxin).
 180 pints of milk (aflatoxin).
 200 gallons of drinking water from Miami or New Orleans.
 90 pounds of broiled steak (cancer risk only).

Smoking
 2 cigarettes

Source: Tables 7-2 to 7-5.

clearly into categories within which intercomparison is more easily justified and probably more accurate. Table 7-2 is a list of various commonplace risks of death, most of which would be considered involuntary. Notice that there may be some overlapping between categories (*home accidents*, for example, includes falls within the home). Table 7-3 shows some occupational risks, mostly risks of fatal accidents. Again, most such risks would be considered involuntary by those exposed. Table 7-4, in contrast, shows a set of voluntary risks of death, those incurred in sporting activities. Table 7-5 is a further set of everyday risks, but now specialized to cancer risks, selected because such risks arouse particularly strong emotions.

Before discussing these risks in more detail and indicating how they are all estimated, we would like to give another example that may help place these risks in perspective. Four tablespoons of peanut butter per day is shown as giving a risk of liver cancer of 8×10^{-6} per year, or a lifetime risk of 6×10^{-4}. But four tablespoons of peanut butter corresponds to 400 kilocalories (Kcal), so if one were to eat only peanut butter, daily energy requirements would be supplied by 26 tablespoons per day, giving a lifetime liver cancer risk of 4×10^{-3}, or 0.004. This should be compared with a lifetime probability of any kind of cancer of about 0.25, even in the absence of peanut butter.

Table 7-2. Some Commonplace Risks of Death in the United States, Based on Estimated U.S. Resident Population (*Source 1*).

Risk	Annual per Capita Risk[a]	Annual Trend[b]	Variability, Percent[c]	Based On	Source
Motor vehicle accident					
Total	2.4×10^{-4}	...	10	1950–78	1
Collision with pedestrian	4.2×10^{-5}	-3.9×10^{-7}	10	1950–78	2
Home accidents[d]	1.1×10^{-4}	-2.9×10^{-6}	5	1950–78	2
Falls	6.2×10^{-5}	-3.0×10^{-6}	6	1963–77	2
Drowning	3.6×10^{-5}	...	7	1963–77	2
Fires	2.8×10^{-5}	-1.0×10^{-6}	5	1963–77	2
Inhalation and ingestion of objects	1.5×10^{-5}	...	10	1968–77	2
Firearms	1.0×10^{-5}	-2.4×10^{-7}	8	1968–77	2
Accidental poisoning					
Gases and vapors	7.7×10^{-6}	...	5	1963–77	2
Solids and liquids (Not drugs or medicaments)	6.0×10^{-6}	...	10	1971–77	2
Electrocution	5.3×10^{-6}	...	5	1971–77	2
Tornadoes	6×10^{-7}	...	100	1950–77	1
Floods	6×10^{-7}	...	100	1950–77	1
Lightning	5×10^{-7}	...	18	1971–77	2
Tropical cyclones and hurricanes	3×10^{-7}	...	160	1952–77	1
Bites and stings by venomous animals and insects	2.4×10^{-7}	...	13	1971–77	2
Air Pollution	2.4×10^{-4}	...		—see text—	

a. Average over indicated years, if no trend is shown. The value of trend line in last year of indicated years is used if a trend is shown.

b. Average annual change of annual per capita risk during years shown. Least squares straight line fit of annual risk versus time. A trend is shown if the estimated trend was significant at the 5 percent level (two-tailed).

c. Estimated standard deviation of annual per capita risk about the trend line (trend) or of the mean value (no trend).

d. Home accidents includes some proportion of some of the following seven risks.

Sources: 1. U.S. Bureau of the Census (1975, Annual).   2. National Safety Council (Annual).

Table 7-3. Some Occupational Risks of Death.

Occupation or Industry	Annual Risk[a]	Annual Trend[b]	Variability, Percent[c]	Based On	Source
Manufacturing	8.2×10^{-5}	-1.6×10^{-6}	8	1955–78	1
Trade	5.3×10^{-5}	-2.3×10^{-6}	15	1955–78	1
Service and government	1.0×10^{-4}	-2.0×10^{-6}	8	1955–78	1
Transport and public utilities	3.7×10^{-4}	...	16	1955–78	1
Agriculture[d]	6.0×10^{-4}	...	9	1955–78	1
Construction	6.1×10^{-4}	-7.0×10^{-6}	6	1955–78	1
Mining and Quarrying	9.5×10^{-4}	...	22	1955–78	1
Farming[e]	3.6×10^{-4}	-5.0×10^{-6}	7	1964–77	1, 2
Tractor fatalities per tractor	8.8×10^{-5}	-1.0×10^{-5}	22	1969–77	1
Metal mining and milling	9.4×10^{-4}	...	15	1959–71	3
Nonmetal mining and milling	7.1×10^{-4}	$+2.3 \times 10^{-5}$	15	1959–71	3
Stone quarries and mills	5.9×10^{-4}	...	20	1959–71	3
Coal mining (accidents)	6.3×10^{-4}	-1.0×10^{-4}	46[f]	1963–77	4
Police officers killed in line of duty					
Total	2.2×10^{-4}	...	19	1975–78	4
By felons	1.3×10^{-4}	-2.1×10^{-5}	8	1975–78	4
Railroad employees	2.4×10^{-4}	-6.0×10^{-6}	7	1963–77	1, 4
Steel worker (accident only)	2.8×10^{-4}	...	?	1969–72	5
Fire fighter	8.0×10^{-4}	...	?	1971–72	5

a. Per person at risk. Average over indicated years, if no trend is shown. The value of trend line in last year of indicated years is used if a trend is shown.

b. Average annual change of annual risk during indicated years. Least squares straight line fit of annual risk versus time. A trend is shown if the estimated trend was significant at the 5 percent level. Note that the error estimates for these trends are generally large.

c. Estimated standard deviation of annual risk about the trend line (trend) or of the mean value (no trend). Expressed as a percentage of the risk shown in the first column.

d. Not strictly comparable with farming category, includes transport accidents and all agriculture.

e. Not strictly comparable with agriculture category, refers to nontransport deaths occurring on farms, the population at risk being assumed to be all employed workers, unpaid family members working more than fifteen hours per week and operators working more than one hour per week.

f. The large variability is due to the bad choice of model (straight line fit) and the large changes occurring in the years indicated.

Sources: 1. National Safety Council (Annual). 2. U.S. Department of Agriculture (1979). 3. U.S. Bureau of Mines (Annual). 4. U.S. Bureau of the Census (Annual). 5. Baldewicz et al. (1974).

Table 7-4. Annual Fatality Risks in Sports.[a]

Sport	Average Annual Risk[b]	Average Annual Deaths	Estimated Population at Risk	Years of Coverage	Source
Aerial acrobatics (professional)	$\lesssim 2 \times 10^{-3}$ d,h	0.22	360	1970-78	1
Air show/air racing and acrobatics	5×10^{-3}	4.9	1,050[c]	1971-77	1
Flying amateur/home built aircraft	3×10^{-3}	25	8,000[c]	1970-77	1
Bicycle racing (registered)	$\lesssim 9 \times 10^{-5}$ d,e	0.33	9,800	1970-78	1
Boating	5×10^{-5}	1,300	27×10^6	1972-78[j]	2, 3
Bobsledding	$\lesssim 7 \times 10^{-4}$ d,f	0	450	1970-78	1
Football					
Sandlot	2×10^{-6}	1.7	10^6	1970-78	1
Professional and Semiprofessional	$\lesssim 4 \times 10^{-4}$ d,g	0.11	1,500	1970-78	1
High school	1×10^{-5l}	13	10^6	1970-78	1
College	3×10^{-5l}	1.2	40,000	1970-78	1
Glider flying	4×10^{-4}	7	18,000[c]	1970-77	1
Hang gliding	$\sim 8 \times 10^{-4}$	31	20,000-60,000	1974-78	1
Hunting	3×10^{-5}	600-800	22×10^6	1972	2, 3
Ice yachting	$\lesssim 1 \times 10^{-4}$ d,h	0.22	4,500-6,500	1970-78	1
Lighter-than-air flying	9×10^{-4}	2.6	3,000[c]	1970-77	1
Mountaineering	6×10^{-4}	34	60,000	1970-78	1
Mountaineering[k]	7×10^{-4}	12	19,000	1951-60	4
Power boat racing	8×10^{-4}	5.2	6,500	1970-78	1
Professional stunting	$\lesssim 1 \times 10^{-2}$ d,i	1	200	1975-78	1
Rodeo	$\lesssim 3 \times 10^{-5}$ d,e	0.33	34,000	1970-78	1

Scuba diving	4×10^{-4}	126	300,000	1970–76	1
Ski racing	2×10^{-5}	2	81,000	1970–78	1
Spelunking	$\lesssim 1 \times 10^{-4}$ d, i	0.44	10,000	1970–78	1
Sport parachuting	2×10^{-3}	41	25,000	1970–78	1
Thoroughbred horseracing	1×10^{-3}	2.6	1,800	1970–78	1
Swimming	3×10^{-5}	2,600	82×10^6	1972–78[j]	2, 3

a. No error estimates are given. The reason is that, although we could give statistical sampling errors on the risks shown, the population size is so uncertain in most cases (by a factor of 2 to 3) that this uncertainty dominates.

b. Per person at risk. See preceding note on error estimates.

c. This population corresponds only to pilots certified by the Federal Aviation Administration.

d. The value shown is statistical 95 percent confidence upper bound, assuming risk proportional to person-years of exposure and a Poisson distribution of deaths. See also note *a* on error estimates.

e. Three deaths observed in time indicated.

f. No deaths observed in time indicated.

g. One death observed in time indicated.

h. Two deaths observed in time indicated.

i. Four deaths observed in time indicated.

j. Population figures from 1972, deaths from 1978. We have assumed a similar population went swimming or boating in 1978.

k. Not strictly comparable with the preceding entry, also labeled *Mountaineering*. The figure in the population column is total man-mountain-days, and the risk is per man-mountain-day. This agrees with the previous figure for annual risk if an average of ~ 0.9 days per year is spent mountaineering, but note that the years of coverage differ also.

l. If participation has remained constant, as we assume, there are possibly decreasing trends in these risks.

Sources: 1. Metropolitan Life Insurance Company (1979). 2. U.S. Bureau of the Census (Annual). 3. National Safety Council (Annual). 4. Ferris (1963). (The article also discusses some of the problems of interpretation of risks such as those shown in this table).

Table 7-5. Everyday Cancer Risks.[a]

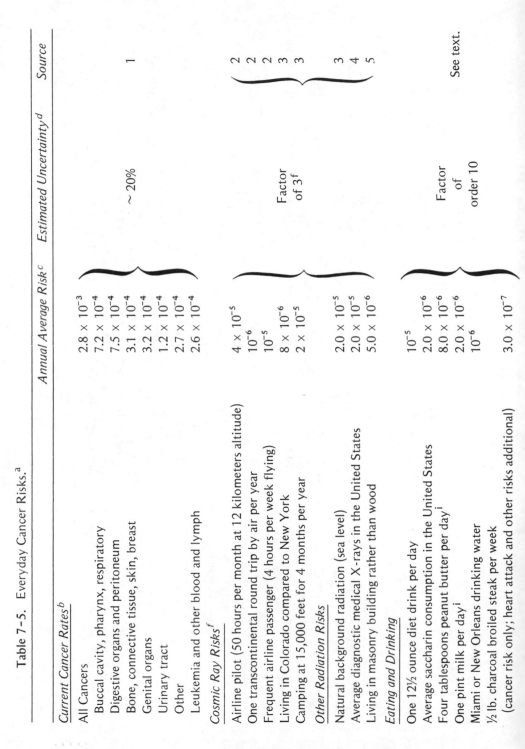

	Annual Average Risk[c]	Estimated Uncertainty[d]	Source
Current Cancer Rates[b]			
All Cancers	2.8×10^{-3}	$\sim 20\%$	1
Buccal cavity, pharynx, respiratory	7.2×10^{-4}		
Digestive organs and peritoneum	7.5×10^{-4}		
Bone, connective tissue, skin, breast	3.1×10^{-4}		
Genital organs	3.2×10^{-4}		
Urinary tract	1.2×10^{-4}		
Other	2.7×10^{-4}		
Leukemia and other blood and lymph	2.6×10^{-4}		
Cosmic Ray Risks[f]			
Airline pilot (50 hours per month at 12 kilometers altitude)	4×10^{-5}	Factor of 3^{f}	2
One transcontinental round trip by air per year	10^{-6}		2
Frequent airline passenger (4 hours per week flying)	10^{-5}		2
Living in Colorado compared to New York	8×10^{-6}		3
Camping at 15,000 feet for 4 months per year	2×10^{-5}		3
Other Radiation Risks			
Natural background radiation (sea level)	2.0×10^{-5}		3
Average diagnostic medical X-rays in the United States	2.0×10^{-5}		4
Living in masonry building rather than wood	5.0×10^{-6}		5
Eating and Drinking			
One 12½ ounce diet drink per day	10^{-5}	Factor of order 10	See text.
Average saccharin consumption in the United States	2.0×10^{-6}		
Four tablespoons peanut butter per day[i]	8.0×10^{-6}		
One pint milk per day[i]	2.0×10^{-6}		
Miami or New Orleans drinking water	10^{-6}		
½ lb. charcoal broiled steak per week (cancer risk only; heart attack and other risks additional)	3.0×10^{-7}		

Alcohol, averaged over smokers and nonsmokers[g]	5.0×10^{-5}	} Factor of order 10	See text.
Alcohol, light drinker (one beer per day)[g]	2.0×10^{-5}		
Tobacco[h]			
Smoker, cancer only	1.2×10^{-3}	} Factor of 3	See text.
Smoker, all effects (including heart disease)	3.0×10^{-3}	Factor of 10	
Person sharing room with smoker	10^{-5}		
Air Pollution			
Polycyclic organics, all effects	1.5×10^{-5}	See text.	See text.

a. These are risks of death, the difference between incidence and mortality being well within the uncertainties shown, (except for the Current Cancer Rates category.

b. Included to give some perspective. The figures given correspond approximately to the lifetime risk divided by the lifetime. The lifetime risk is estimated by the fraction of those dying who die of the given cancer, average lifetime is estimated as seventy years. Since cancer rates increase rapidly with age and the population age structure is changing, these figures are only approximate. Data from *Vital Statistics of the United States*, 1975.

c. Averaged over the whole population of the United States.

d. Even the uncertainties in these estimates can be very large. The uncertainties are mostly estimated subjectively and are conditional on the models used for extrapolation being approximately correct.

e. Averaged over males and females. The risk is approximately double for females only.

f. We assume a linear model with a total of 1 cancer per 5,000 man-rem, corresponding to BEIR 1972. More recent estimates of the BEIR committee (1980) would give slightly lower estimates.

g. Cirrhosis of the liver. Not a cancer, but included here since the methods used are similar. It is possible that in this case there is a threshold effect for damage. In addition there is some evidence that moderate alcohol consumption is associated with lower death rates from other diseases.

h. Based on human data.

i. Based on human data for aflatoxin carcinogenicity. Note that we assume that the measured aflatoxins are aflatoxin B, the most potent. If some corresponds to other aflatoxins, these estimated risks should be reduced.

Sources: (The following references are the sources of data used in the models. We have estimated the risks). 1. U.S. Department of Health, Education and Welfare (1975). 2. United Nations Scientific Committee on the Effects of Atomic Radiation (UNSCEAR) (1962). 3. Oakley (1972). 4. United Nations Scientific Committee on the Effects of Atomic Radiation (UNSCEAR) (1977). We have used the bone marrow dose here. 5. Moeller and Underhill (1976).

Calculation of Risks

The magnitudes of the risks in Tables 7-2 through 7-5 have been evaluated in various ways, depending on the availability of data (see Chapter 3), and the measure of risk employed is the average probability of death (see Chapter 2). Evaluating risks such as those in Tables 7-2 and 7-3 is straightforward, because estimates are based on historical statistics. All that is required is a knowledge of the numbers killed in the past and the populations at risk, the sources of data for which are indicated on the tables. An exception to this is the estimation of the risk due to air pollution (from sulfates; the cancer risk from benzo(α)pyrene is dealt with subsequently), which was mentioned also in Chapter 2.

The effect of sulfur oxides on human beings is mostly irritation of the bronchial tract. Careful laboratory measurements on animals show that the resistance to bronchial air flow in guinea pigs is in direct proportion to the sulfate concentration, but the sulfates (sulfuric acid, zinc ammonium sulfate) that are prevalent in power plant plumes are more important than others that come from natural causes (sodium sulfate) or pure sulfur dioxide.

There are also some large-scale human epidemiological surveys. A study shows that incidence of bronchitis in seven Japanese cities (Nishiwaki et al. 1971) is proportional to the sulfate level, and Lave and Seskin (1970) show the same effect for the mortality rate in the United States. The numerical calculation has been confirmed by a recalculation of the same data (Hamilton 1974). In Norway, the death rate in 156 winter weeks shows a linear relation with the SO_2 concentration (Lindbergh 1968). Finally, the CHESS studies from the Environmental Protection Agency (EPA) (Finklea et al. 1975) show health effects at sulfate levels as low as 10 micrograms per cubic meter, whereas the sulfate level in eastern cities is 20 micrograms per cubic meter. These data are consistent with a linear relation between mortality and sulfate concentrations, with no threshold above the ambient levels, the relation used to obtain the estimate shown in Table 7-2. A review of such health effects has been made by Wilson et al. (1980).

Recreational risks such as those in Table 7-4 are much harder to quantify, largely because they are so variable. Again, the sources of the estimates of these risks are included in the table. It must be realized that the uncertainties in these estimates are much larger than in the previous two tables because of the difficulty in estimating numbers and exposure of those at risk, although the total number of deaths is usually reasonably well known.

To illustrate, consider the risk of death from bear attack in or near Glacier National Park. In the last fifteen years there have been five cases (1/3 per year). If this number is averaged over the 1.6 million yearly park visitors, the risk is seen to be very small. But the deaths have all been among backpackers, who are 200 times fewer in number. In this group the risk is thus 200 times greater, although still about the same as driving a car 1,200 miles and so perhaps comparable to the risk in driving to and from the park. It might be possible to identify a specific characteristic of backpackers that places them at risk and so to identify a smaller group at maximum risk, but this would require data much harder to obtain.

The evaluation of the cancer risks of Table 7-5 presents the greatest challenge, so we discuss them in more detail. Each case is treated using the model outlined in Chapter 3. A linear relation is assumed between dose of or exposure to a carcinogen, and the response. When human epidemiology is not available, we use animal data and assume that human beings, if given the same daily dose relative to body weight as animals, would acquire, on average, the same number of cancers in their lifetimes as the animals acquired on average in theirs. To some extent, therefore, these risks are hypothetical.

Radiation

Radiation cancers have been studied in human beings and animals. We take the numbers here from the first report of the Committee on Biological Effects of Ionizing Radiation (BEIR I) of the National Academy of Sciences (National Academy of Sciences 1972) which uses a linear interpolation for low doses. (A more recent report (known as BEIR III) of this committee (NAS 1980) suggests that this proportional relation is too pessimistic.) Cross-country airplanes travel at an altitude of about 35,000 feet (10 kilometers), at which height there is an appreciable radiation dose due to cosmic radiation, including neutrons. To estimate this we use the report of the United

Nations Scientific Committee on the Effects of Atomic Radiation (see UNSCEAR 1962: 201, figure 1).[1] The dose at a latitude of 55° N is 2,000 millirems/year of ionizing radiation and 3,600 millirems/year of neutrons, although these doses will be markedly higher during periods of solar flares.

A 5-hour transcontinental flight at an altitude of 10 kilometers gives a total dose between 3 and 4 millirems. Using the relationship between cancer incidence and whole body dose in the BEIR report, we find a cancer risk of 5×10^{-7} per transcontinental flight. This is smaller than (1/6 of) the risk of accident and is normally neglected in any discussion of the risks of airplane travel. But it is derived on a basis comparable to the cancer risks discussed here and helps to put them in perspective.

The doses from diagnostic X rays, from buildings and so on, are obtainable from various places such as the UNSCEAR reports and the BEIR I report.

Saccharin

As discussed in Chapter 6, 2,500 milligrams per kilogram per day of saccharin in the diet of rats led to a 24 percent incidence of bladder tumors. Each 12½ ounce diet drink contains ~ 150 milligrams of saccharin, so one diet drink per day for human beings is 150 per 70 milligrams per kilogram per day, giving a lifetime risk of cancer of 2×10^{-4}, or an annual average risk of 3×10^{-6}.

Drinking Water

The principal carcinogen in drinking water is chloroform produced by action of chlorine in water purification systems on organic matter (Morris 1975). Chlorination is performed, of course, to remove the far higher risk of spreading disease through the water supply.

A survey of concentrations by the Environmental Protection Agency (1977) found concentrations of 200 parts per million in drinking water of Miami and New Orleans. The risk can be calculated

1. It might be thought that the neutrons would be absorbed by the airplane and the body. Since they are in equilibrium with the surrounding air, this can be allowed for by taking the dose at a lower altitude, but the effect is small.

directly from data on rats and mice or can be obtained from a National Academy of Sciences (NAS) report (Advisory Committee on Toxicology 1977) in which the lifetime risk (upper limit, 95 percent confidence) is calculated as 3.7×10^{-7} for 1 microgram per liter concentration in water. Taking their upper limit as a best estimate leads to 6×10^{-9}/year for 1 microgram per liter, or 1.2×10^{-6} annual average risk at 200 parts per million in drinking water.

We assume that the NAS calculations refer to ordinary intake of water and that cancers at other than the primary site are taken into account. Although this calculation applies only to the chloroform in the water, the other carcinogens present may be dealt with in a similar way. Using the concentrations found by the EPA, however, shows that chloroform poses the major hazard, since the more potent carcinogens are present only at very low concentrations.

Air Pollution

Polluted air contains many carcinogens. One that has been identified and is frequently monitored is benzo(α)pyrene. Other polycyclic organic compounds are probably carcinogenic, but they have not all been monitored.

If we make the assumption—reasonable for a rough calculation and in any case all we can do—that all burning processes produce the carcinogenic polycyclic hydrocarbons in equal proportions, then monitoring benzo(α)pyrene can give us a relative hazard index. This can be made into an absolute hazard index by epidemiological studies in which the increase of lung cancer (among nonsmokers) is tentatively attributed to polycyclic hydrocarbons with benzo(α)pyrene as an index. Such studies are compared in a review (Pike et al. 1975) that states that it is prudent to assume that breathing air with an average concentration of 10 nanograms per cubic meter is equivalent to smoking one cigarette a day. This "match" was made for lung cancer; but because of the similarities between cigarette smoking and air pollution, we assume that the other problems of cigarette smoking, such as other cancers, including bladder cancer, and heart disease, also occur with polycyclic organic matter in the same proportion. We showed earlier that the average risk from cigarette smoking in the United States is about 0.5×10^{-6} per cigarette or about 2×10^{-4} per year for one cigarette per day.

Even as late as 1970, many American cities had outdoor ambient benzo(α)pyrene concentrations of 1.5 nanograms per cubic meter, giving a yearly risk of 3×10^{-5}. Indoors the concentration is less, leading to an overall risk one-half this amount.

Comparisons of the amount of benzo(α)pyrene breathed in with the results of animal experiments in which it is fed to animals would suggest lower risks than the estimate just given, but the fact that benzo(α)pyrene is merely an indicator for other carcinogens upsets the comparison, and the human effect is larger than a naive use of the animal data would suggest.

Charcoal Broiling Steaks

It has been noted that many carcinogens are produced in detectable amounts when steaks are charcoal broiled. Char-broiled chicken and broiled fish are also covered with carcinogens. These can come from the charcoal, for it is well known that burning carbonaceous materials produces carcinogens—the first cases of environmental carcinogenesis noted by Percival Potts 200 years ago were associated with the burning of coal—or they can come from pyrolization of the meat at high temperature.

Lijinsky and Shubik (1974) noted over a dozen potential carcinogens from broiling steaks. We use only the best known, benzo(α)pyrene, for this calculation, which is therefore a lower limit. Nine micrograms is present in a 1-kilogram (2-pound) steak or 2 micrograms for 1/2 pound steak. Data on Chinese hamsters ingesting benzo(α)pyrene daily for a lifetime indicate a potency such that there is induction of tumors in 50 percent of the animals for 100 micrograms ingested per kilogram body weight per day. Extrapolating to human beings eating 1/2 pound broiled steak per week gives an annual average risk of 3×10^{-7}. This cancer risk is very small, and eating charcoal broiled steaks to excess will give far higher risks of other problems, such as heart disease.

Aflatoxin

Aflatoxin, produced by mold and appearing extensively in nature, is a potent carcinogen. Several aflatoxins often occur together; we will consider them together and quote only results for aflatoxin B1 where such specificity is required. Although molds occur naturally, their growth may be controlled, and so the concentration of aflatoxin in foods may be controlled by society. Careful storage of grain and elimination of peanuts with cracked shells serves to reduce concentrations.

Epidemiological studies (Peers and Linsell 1973, Shank et al. 1972, Van Rensberg et al. 1974) in man and animal experiments, (Butler and Barnes 1968; Butler, Greenblatt, and Lijinsky 1969; Wogan, Papliolunga, and Newbreme 1974), indicate a lifetime human risk of liver cancer of 3×10^{-7} for 0.1 micrograms per day human ingestion. The U.S. Food and Drug Administration (1974) has summarized available data on aflatoxin and suggests that the average concentration in peanut butter was about 3 parts per billion at that time, the action level then being set at 20 parts per billion.

Assuming these figures, 4 tablespoons (64 grams) of peanut butter contains 0.14 micrograms aflatoxin, so 4 tablespoons per day results in a lifetime risk of liver cancer of 6×10^{-4}, an average annual risk of 8×10^{-6}. A survey of milk (*Food Chemical News* 1977) found aflatoxin levels of 0.1 parts per billion and above in 177 of 302 samples, or roughly half. An average level might thus be 0.1 parts per billion, so that 1 pint (~ 500 grams) per day of milk gives an annual average risk of 2×10^{-6}.

Alcohol and Cirrhosis

The cases of cirrhosis of the liver are assumed to be entirely due to alcohol consumption, at a rate we assume to be proportional to the consumption. This is suggested by a World Health Organization (WHO) study comparing data for fourteen countries, with average annual per capita intake varying from 4 to 25 liters. A very high correlation was found between cirrhosis rates and alcohol consumption rates. This does not prove that consumers of moderate quantities of alcohol have a proportionate risk of cirrhosis. It may merely be that the number of alcoholics or heavy drinkers is proportional to the total countrywide consumption. In the United States the cirrhosis rate in 1974 was 2.1×10^{-4} per year for men and 1.1×10^{-4} per year for women, the difference being consistent with the relative alcohol consumption of men and women, or an average of 1.6×10^{-4} per year.

The evidence for carcinogenicity of alcohol is confusing. It is unclear whether alcohol functions as a carcinogen, cocarcinogen, or through an indirect mechanism such as alteration of bacterial flow through the gastrointestinal tract. Moreover, some or all of any effect may be due to impurities in the beer or wine. But for our purposes, these caveats do not matter. People drink beer or wine, impurities and all, and the intake is large enough that it is almost certainly above any threshold. But there is, for oral cancer at least, a very strong synergism between smoking and alcohol. There have been correlations between cancer and alcohol intake also for the mouth, pharynx, larynx, esophagus, liver, and possibly rectum.

Rothman (1977) estimates the overall risk as follows. In 1968, 14,454 cancers occurred at sites with which alcohol has been associated. This gives a risk of 7×10^{-5} per year. These are probably concentrated in the 20 percent of heavy drinkers (who are usually also smokers) to give them a risk of 2×10^{-4} per year.

The average beer consumption in the United States is 2/3 pints per day with approximately double this amount of alcohol consumed in wine and spirits. A light drinker (1 pint of beer per day only) still has a risk of cirrhosis of 7×10^{-5} per year.

We must stress here that alcohol has many effects on people in addition to those discussed. It is implicated in many automobile accidents, and alcoholism causes many problems other than cirrhosis. The numbers here are therefore lower limits on the total risks of imbibing alcohol.

Uncertainties

> Round numbers are always false.
>
> Samuel Johnson. 30 March 1778. In Boswell's
> Life of Johnson, Vol. iii, p. 226.

The reader will note that in addition to the estimates of risks given in Tables 7–2 through 7–5 there are estimates of the uncertainties. For Tables 7–2 and 7–3 these uncertainties may be derived from historical data, for we are using models that assume that current trends will continue. In Table 7–5, on cancer risks, the uncertainty estimates are both much larger and also much more difficult to make. Usually they correspond to a factor of about 3 for uncertainties in estimating how potent the various carcinogens are from human data, together with an estimate of the uncertainty in dose of carcinogen. In estimating potency from animal data, the uncertainty is less (the experiments are better controlled), but there is then an uncertainty of a factor of 3 or 4 in extrapolating from animals to humans, in addition to the uncertainties in dose.

REFERENCES

Amdur, M.O. 1973. "Animal Studies." In *Proceedings of the Conference on Health Effects of Air Pollutants.* National Academy of Sciences, National Research Council Assembly of Life Sciences. Washington, D.C., October 3-5.

_____. 1971. "Aerosols Formed by Oxidation of Sulfur Dioxide. Review of their Toxicology." *Archives of Environmental Health* 23: 459.

_____. 1968. "Toxicological Appraisal of Particulate Matter, Oxides of Sulfur and Sulfuric Acid." *Journal of the Air Pollution Control Association* 14: 638.

Baldewicz, W.; G. Haddock; V. Lee; Prajoto; R. Whitley; and V. Denny. 1974. "Historical Perspectives on Risk for Large Scale Technological Systems." Unpublished report, UCLA–ENG–7485, University of California.

Butler, W., and J. Barnes. 1968. "Carcinogenic Action of Ground Nutmeal Containing Aflatoxin in Rats." *Food and Cosmetics Toxicology* 6: 135.

Butler, W.; M. Greenblatt; and W. Lijinsky. 1969. "Carcinogenesis in Rats by Aflatoxins B1, G1, and B2." *Cancer Research* 29: 220.

Department of Health, Education and Welfare. 1979. *Smoking and Health.* A Report of the Surgeon General. Washington, D.C.: U.S. Government Printing Office.

Doll, R., and A.B. Hill. 1964. *British Medical Journal* 1: 1399.

Environmental Protection Agency. 1977. *National Organics Monitoring Survey.* Washington, D.C.

Ferris, B.G. 1963. *New England Journal of Medicine* 268: 430.

Food Chemical News. 1977. (November 28): 38.

_____. 1977. (November 7): 22.

Hamilton, L.D. (ed.). 1974. Report from the Biomedical and Environmental Assessment Group. BNL 20582, July 30, Brookhaven National Laboratory, Upton, New York.

Lave, L., and E. Seskin. 1970. "Air Pollution and Human Health." *Science* 169: 723.

Lijinsky, W., and P. Shubik. 1964. "Benzo(α)pyrene and Other Polynuclear Hydrocarbons in Charcoal-Broiled Meat." *Science* 145: 53.

Lindbergh, W. 1968. "Der Alminnilige luft forurensing i norse." ("General Air Pollution in Norway.") Oslo: Utgit av Royksderadit (Smoke Damage Council).

Metropolitan Life Insurance Company. 1979. *Statistical Bulletin* 60 (no. 3, July–September).

Moeller, D.W., and D.W. Underhill. 1976. "Final Report on Study of the Effects of Building Materials on Population Dose Equivalents." Harvard School of Public Health, December.

Morris, J.C. 1975. "Formation of Halogenated Hydrocarbons by Chlorination—A Review." Report to the Environmental Protection Agency, PB 241511, Harvard University, March.

National Academy of Sciences. 1972. *The Effects on Populations of Exposure to Low Levels of Ionizing Radiations.* Report of the Advisory Committee on the Biological Effects of Ionizing Radiations (BEIR 1).

National Safety Council. Annual. *Accident Facts.* Chicago, Illinois.

Oakley, D.T. 1972. *Natural Radiation Exposure in the U.S.* U.S. Environmental Protection Agency report ORP/SID 72-1. Washington, D.C.

Pike, M.C. et al. 1975. "Air Pollution." Chapter 14 in *Persons at High Risk of Cancer: An Approach to Cancer Etiology and Control,* edited by J.F. Fraumeni. New York: Academic Press.

Preston, S.H.; N. Keyfitz; and R. Schoen. 1972. *Causes of Death—Life Tables For National Populations.* New York: Seminar Press.

Nishiwaki, Y.; Y. Tsunetoshi; T. Shimizu; M. Ueda; N. Nakayama; H. Takahashi; A. Ichinosawa; S. Kajihara; A. Ohshino; M. Ogino; and K. Sakaki. 1971. "Atmospheric Contamination of Industrial Areas Including Fossil-fuel Power Stations, and a Method of Evaluating Possible Effects on Inhabitants." Vienna: International Atomic Energy Agency, IAEA–SM–146/16.

Peers, F., and C. Linsell. 1973. "Dietary Aflatoxins and Liver Cancer: A Population Based Study in Kenya." *British Journal of Cancer* 27: 473.

Rothman, K.J. 1977. Chapter 9 in *Persons at High Risk of Cancer: An Approach to Cancer Etiology and Control,* edited by J.F. Fraumeni. New York: Academic Press.

Schwing, R.C. 1979. "Longevity Benefits and Costs of Reducing Various Risks." *Technological Forecasting and Social Change* 13: 333.

Shank, R.; J. Gordon; E. Wogan; A. Nondasuta; and B. Subhamani. 1972. "Dietary Aflatoxins and Human Liver Cancer III: Field Survey of Rural Thai Families for Ingested Aflatoxins." *Food and Cosmetics Toxicology* 10: 71.

United Nations Scientific Committee on the Effects of Atomic Radiation (UNSCEAR). 1977. Report to the General Assembly. New York: United Nations.

_____. 1962. Report to the General Assembly. New York: United Nations.

U.S. Bureau of Mines. Annual. *Minerals Yearbook.* Washington, D.C.

U.S. Bureau of the Census. 1975. *Historical Statistics of the United States, Colonial Times to 1970.* Washington, D.C.

_____. Annual. *The Statistical Abstract of the United States.* Washington, D.C.

U.S. Department of Agriculture. 1979. *Agricultural Statistics.* Washington, D.C.

U.S. Department of Health, Education and Welfare. 1975. *Vital Statistics of the United States.* Maryland: National Center for Health Statistics.

U.S. Food and Drug Administration. 1974. *Federal Register*, December 6, 39FR42748.

Van Rensberg, S.; J. Van der Watt; I. Purchase; L. Pereira Coutinko; and L. Markham. 1974. "Primary Liver Cancer Rate and Aflatoxin Intake in a High Cancer Area." *South African Medical Journal* 38: 2808a.

Wilson, R.; S.D. Colome; J.D. Spengler; and D.G. Wilson. 1980. *Health Effects of Fossil Fuel Burning.* Cambridge, Massachusetts: Ballinger Publishing Company.

Wogan, G.; S. Papliolunga; and P. Newbreme. 1974. "Carcinogenic Effects of Low Dietary Levels of Aflatoxin B1 in Rats." *Food and Cosmetics Toxicology* 12: 681.

8 MANAGING AND REDUCING RISKS

In skating over thin ice, safety is our speed.

Ralph Waldo Emerson, Essays vii.

The purpose of analyzing risks is not only to reassure ourselves that we are not engaging in any activity that is unusually dangerous, but also to enable us to concentrate efforts to reduce unusually large risks at the appropriate point in the cause–effect chain. By this means we hope to steadily reduce risk in society. In Chapter 3 it was mentioned that some risks are obviously too large to be acceptable and others too small to be worth discussing. The catalogue of risks in Chapter 7 allows the range of risks to be defined more clearly.

Management of risks has followed three roughly separable procedures.

1. Ban the activity, process, or material.

2. Reduce the activity or exposure to the pollutant as much as possible without causing bankruptcy.

3. Conduct a thorough risk/benefit analysis, to allow a fuller appreciation of all the factors involved. Use the results as a guide for action to manage the risks.

It is the last procedure we espouse in this book, with a very strong emphasis on the word *thorough*. It was shown in Chapter 6 that several attempts to perform risk/benefit analysis have been inadequate. If time, knowledge, and resources do not admit of a thorough analysis, sometimes one of the other approaches might be justifiable.

The first approach—a ban—was used by many primitive societies, in which many activities were subject to taboo. As societies developed, the taboos changed. In this context, an important difference exists between the risks we are concerned about today and the risks of past centuries. One hundred years ago, many risks, as from tuberculosis and contaminated water supplies, were large, so that when the causes were recognized, the risks could be almost completely eliminated at modest cost, both financial and in the sense of introducing new risks, and in an obvious fashion. Nowadays society is concerned about many smaller risks that are expensive, possibly in both senses, to eliminate completely. The Delaney amendment to the Food and Drug Acts of 1950 can be considered a modern taboo. At the time of its enactment, cancer was even less well understood than it is now, and few human carcinogens were recognized, only cigarettes, β-naphthylamine, and radiation. Moreover, the analytical methods for detecting small quantities of pollutants were not developed, and impurities could be detected only at a level of one part per million or so. Any chemical known to be carcinogenic was, in the terminology of Chapter 4, a potent carcinogen. If it was detectable, it must have been present at levels of one part per million or more, so that the risk of cancer from frequent use worked out to be high (10^{-5} per year or more). It therefore seemed scientifically very sensible to ban all such chemicals and, if it became necessary to allow a carcinogen, to handle it on a case-by-case basis in Congress. Twenty-eight chemicals are now known to be carcinogens in human beings and several hundred more in animals and, by implication, in human beings. In several cases if the Delaney clause were strictly applied the results would be absurd. Aflatoxin B1 is a potent carcinogen present in milk, corn, and nut products, as noted in Chapter 7; to reduce aflatoxin as much as possible seems wise, but to ban any products containing any detectable quantity appears excessive. This is a slightly artificial example, because aflatoxin is not a food additive in the sense of the Delaney clause, though it conforms to the spirit of the clause. It can be seen from such examples that any ban or taboo should be reexamined every decade or so to be sure that the original information or lack of it justifying the taboo is still up to date.

A case can still be made for the Delaney clause as applied to additives deliberately added to foods. Additives are added to be tasted, smelled, seen, or to preserve. For each of these purposes a fractional amount of about 1 in 10,000 is necessary. For a common food, possibly representing up to 10 percent of the diet, the additive might thus represent 1 in 100,000 (10^{-5}) of the diet. When carcinogenicity is measured in rodents typically fifty animals are used at each dose level tested. Carcinogenicity can just be detected if 10 percent of these animals develop cancer in their lifetimes as a consequence of addition of suspected carcinogen to their diet, but the material—even if nontoxic—can be added only to a level of about 10 percent of their diet. If, as is often assumed, carcinogenicity is proportional to dose, the number of cancers at the lower (human) dose of 1 in 100,000 would be (10 percent) $\times$ (10^{-5}/10 percent) per animal per lifetime, or about 1 in 100,000. (Note that this method of calculation differs somewhat from that used in Chapter 4, where equivalent human effects were assumed for doses that represented similar fractions of body weights of humans and animals. In the present case equivalent human effects are assumed for an equal fraction in the diet, an assumption that may overestimate the human effects if the other assumption is actually correct.)

The uncertainties in deriving human experience from animal data were described in Chapter 4. If people are as sensitive in their lifetimes as animals in theirs, however, this is a lifetime risk of 10^{-5}, or an annual risk of 1.5×10^{-7} averaged over all persons; with 225 million population, this risk would mean thirty cancers per year in the United States. Some groups of heavy users would be at much larger risk.

Having made this case for possible retention of the Delaney clause for deliberate food additives, we note that the U.S. Congress has firmly rejected its use in the one clear case where it was applicable! (That is saccharin; see Chapter 6.) This seems inconsistent. Consistency may be the refuge of small minds, but we feel it is the duty of a risk analyst to point out inconsistencies so that if they are retained they are retained deliberately.

The second type of hazard management, reducing a pollutant as much as possible short of bankruptcy, may be useful in certain situations. The U.S. Occupational Health and Safety Administration (OSHA) wanted carcinogens to be reduced to the lowest feasible level; the Clean Air Acts administered by the Environmental Protection Agency demand that (in so-called "nonattainment" areas where air quality is lower than the legislated standards) there be the lowest achievable emission rate (LEAR). In all areas the best available control technology (BACT) must be used. Listed in Chapter 7 are a death rate and a risk due to living in urban polluted air typical of the eastern half of the United States (Chicago—Boston—New York—Washington, D.C.). We noted that large uncertainty arises from differences of opinion in the assessment of this risk. The suggested death rate of 50,000 per year is large. If society believes $5 million should be spent to save a life, $250 billion would have to be spent to prevent those deaths—a huge amount of money, impossible to spend without large-scale bankruptcies. In such circumstances, almost any amount short of bankruptcy seems reasonable.

The principle of best available technology has already been applied, successfully and with common sense, to water pollution. The legislation demands pure water almost independent of cost, but it sets no risk limit. It would be possible to distill water at considerable cost, but water supplies are merely chlorinated (and sometimes filtered), and there has been no legal objection to stopping technology short at this point. In this case, the cost difference between the two technical mitigation methods, chlorination and distillation, was so great that no detailed risk/cost/benefit analysis was necessary to decide between them. However, we note that several organic carcinogens appear in drinking water, among them chloroform, which appeared in the catalogue of risks in Chapter 7; it will need sophisticated analysis to decide whether and how much to remove the chloroform.

We believe that a thorough risk/cost/benefit analysis is the best way of deciding procedures. It seems logical, however, to use the less sophisticated management methods, banning or best available technology, until someone has done a risk/cost/benefit analysis. Who decides when the analysis is good enough to replace the cruder approach? Presumably the legislature and the courts do. The U.S. Supreme Court, in reviewing in 1980 the court of appeals decision to disallow a tightening of occupational exposure to benzene, seemed to follow this logic.

It had been noted by OSHA that benzene exposures have caused leukemia and that such exposures thus pose a risk, albeit a hypothetical one, even at low concentrations. OSHA proposed that the concentration limit in the workplace be reduced from ten parts per million to the lowest feasible level, which was arbitrarily determined to be one part per million. No risk/cost/benefit analysis was carried out. Evidence was presented showing that no leukemia had been attributed to exposures at ten parts per million so that any adverse health effect must be hypothetical—just such as needs a risk analysis. The risk may be estimated from data at higher doses by assuming proportionality, and is comparable to other occupational risks and smaller than many; it can thus be considered insignificant.

A majority of the U.S. Supreme Court held that the U.S. secretary of labor had not "found" that the risk was significant and, by quoting the risk assessment, implied that it might reasonably be used to discuss the significance. We hope that this decision of the Supreme Court will be viewed in the following logical light: Management methods 1 and 2, banning and best available control technology, should be regarded as stopgap measures of risk management to be replaced whenever a good risk benefit analysis is performed.

Fault tree analyses for failure probabilities and event tree analyses for failure scenarios have been used within industrial and engineering companies for reliability assessment and improvement. Such analyses are known there as reliability analysis. In the example we selected in Chapter 6, Rasmussen's report on nuclear reactor safety, the use of the event tree analysis enabled a common mode failure to be identified and removed from the particular reactor studied (Surry I). If the event tree procedure had been applied to other reactors, particularly those of a different manufacturer (Babcock and Wilcox), the different control system would have been noted and probably the Three Mile Island accident would have been averted. A mandatory study of the risk of each such technology may be appropriate, with the aim of reducing risk.

Even though a risk/benefit analysis might lead to acceptance of a technology, that technology should constantly be improved to reduce risk. To hasten technology improvement, which is often very slow, it seems worthwhile to find incentives and procedures. Following are three examples.

1. X rays were discovered in 1897, and very soon thereafter their use for medical diagnosis began. Almost at once some adverse effects were discovered; skin cancers were the first to be observed, but other cancers were discovered among radium dial painters in the 1920s.

Although the risk of using X rays was well known, physicians stated their view, which is generally agreed to be correct, that the benefit of prompt diagnosis outweighed the possible risks. Yet the identical benefit can be obtained with less risk by reducing the X-ray exposure. It has long been known how to do this by using better X-ray film, intensifying screens, and shielding, but it took nearly thirty years for the reduction of risk to be achieved. Even as late as 1950, the X-ray exposure of chest examinations was 1 roentgen, 140 times greater than the 7 milliroentgens commonly used today.

2. Pesticides and herbicides have enabled food production in the United States to increase considerably since 1940. The increase in well-being, including reduction of risk of death from starvation and disease is considerable, and is usually considered to outweigh the risks of the pesticides by a wide margin. But that is not the whole story. In her famous book *Silent Spring* (1962) Rachel Carson pointed out that there is a lot of unnecessary use of pesticides and that the same benefit of improved crops can be obtained with less risk by using a little care.

3. Many scientists believe that the proposal of FDA to ban saccharin in prepared foods was foolish; they compare the risk of saccharin and the risk of sugar. Most Americans are overweight, a condition that leads to many problems including increased probability of cancer. If the choice is between more saccharin as a sweetener and more sugar as a sweetener, it should be considered that increased sugar poses a risk ten times greater. But those are not the only two possible choices. We can think at once of two more: not to use a sweetener at all and to return to the use of cyclamates, which may have been banned for incorrect reasons.

The three examples have a common feature: The risk/benefit comparison is too narrowly posed. By posing the questions more broadly we can reduce the overall risk to society. These examples must not be used to discredit risk/benefit analysis. Diagnostic X rays and pesticides were worth having, and the decision to use them was, in our view, correctly taken. We do believe, however, that society must constantly look for new technological alternatives that can reduce risk.

No rigorous analytical procedure exists for finding new technological procedures. However, the very act of performing a risk assessment often suggests ways of reducing risk, such as those available in reactor safety by using Rasmussen's event tree techniques. We suggest therefore that technology improvement can be maintained by repeating a risk/benefit analysis on major technologies at regular intervals.

An alternative espoused by the U.S. Congress (in the automobile emission standards, for example) has been to mandate a reduction of risk by a definite time. This is similar in its effect to the demanding best available control technology and is a less sensitive tool (although easier) than repeated risk/benefit analyses.

Another alternative is to provide incentives. In capitalist society the obvious incentive is money, perhaps in the form of a risk fee — or pollution charge — on any risk in society. This might be at a level of $1 to $10 million per life saved or $1 to $10 for a risk of one in a million. Then there would be continuous financial incentive to reduce the fee by reducing the risk. Such financial incentives do not guarantee that methods of risk reduction will be discovered but may help. Financial incentives, although attractive to most economists, are unattractive politically. Nonetheless, we suggest that risk fee be calculated as a useful guide to the regulator to see if his other regulation methods make sense or not.

Finally we note here that summaries have been compiled (see Chapters 4 and 5) of the amounts society has been willing to pay to save lives. In many cases the amounts are to save a life by medical treatment, which is not risk reduction as the term is used here. In other cases, however, the amount is for direct risk reduction. We note especially the increasing use of the risk assessment by the National Highway Safety Administration (NHTSA) in deciding how much to spend on road safety improvements.

REFERENCE

Carson, R. 1962. *Silent Spring.* New York: Fawcett Publications, Inc.

BIBLIOGRAPHY

This bibliography is a highly abridged and updated version of that issued as an informal report (BNL 22285-R) by the Biomedical and Environmental Assessment Division, National Center for Analysis of Energy Systems, Brookhaven National Laboratory, Associated Universities, Inc., Upton, New York 11973. That report was prepared by Elizabeth M. Clark and Andrew J. Van Horn, with later modifications by Laura Hedal and Edmund A. C. Crouch.

None of the references given at the ends of the preceeding chapters are duplicated in this bibliography.

Abelson, P. H. 1973. "Consumer Product Safety." *Science* 179: 17.

Ackerman, B.; S. Rose-Ackerman; J. W. Sawyer; and D. W. Henderson. 1974. *The Uncertain Search for Environmental Quality.* New York: The Free Press.

Altschuler, B. 1970. "Theory for the Measurement of Competing Risks in Animal Experiments." *Mathematical Biosciences* 6: 1-11.

Altzinger, E.; M. Brook; J. Wilbert; M. R. Chernick; B. Elsner; and W. V. Foster. 1972. *Compendium on Risk Analysis Techniques.* Aberdeen Proving Grounds, Maryland: U.S. Army Material Systems Analysis Agency Special Publication Number 4.

Arrow, K. J., and A. C. Fisher. 1974. "Environmental Preservation, Uncertainty and Irreversibility." *Quarterly Journal of Economics* 88: 312-319.

Ashford, N. A. 1975. *Crisis in the Workplace: Occupational Disease and Injury, a Report to the Ford Foundation.* Cambridge, Massachusetts: MIT Press.

Baker, R. F.; R.M. Michels; and E. Preston. 1975. *Public Policy Development: Linking the Technical and Political Processes.* New York: John Wiley and Sons.

Baram, M. S. 1976. "Regulation of Environmental Carcinogens: Why Cost–Benefit Analysis May be Harmful to Your Health." *Technology Review* 78, no. 8 (July/August): 40–43.

Baram, M. S. 1973. "Technology Assessment and Social Control." *Science* 180: 465–473.

Barlow, R. E., and P. Chatterjee. 1973. *Introduction to Fault Tree Analysis.* Berkeley, California: Operations Research Center, University of California,

Barrager, S.; B. R. Judd; and D. W. North. 1976, "The Economic and Social Costs of Coal and Nuclear Electrical Generation: A Framework for Assessment and Illustrative Calculations for the Coal and Nuclear Fuel Cycles." A discussion paper prepared for an Environmental Workshop held at MITRE Corporation, May 27–28, 1975. SRI Project MSU–4133.

Baumol, W. J., and W. E. Oates. 1975. *The Theory of Environmental Policy: Externalities, Public Outlays and Quality of Life.* Englewood Cliffs, New Jersey: Prentice–Hall.

Baxter, W. F. 1974. *People or Penguines: The Case for Optimal Pollution.* New York: Columbia University Press.

Boffey, P. M. 1971. "Radiation Standards: Are the Right People Making Decisions." *Science* 171: 780–783.

Bowen, J. J. 1975. "The Choice of Criteria for Individual Risk, for Statistical Risks, and for Public Risk." In *Risk–Benefit Methodology and Application* (UCLA–ENG–7598), edited by D. Okrent. Los Angeles: School of Engineering and Applied Sciences, University of California.

Bunker, J. P.; B. A. Barnes; and F. Mosteller, eds. 1977. *Costs, Risks and Benefits of Surgery.* New York: Oxford University Press.

Burton, I.; R. Kates; and G. White. 1975. *The Environment as Hazard.* Cambridge, Massachusetts: MIT Press.

Butzel, A. K. 1972. "Legal Mechanisms for Risk–Benefit Analysis: Some Thoughts on the Significance of the Storm King Case." In *Perspectives on Benefit–Risk Decision Making.* Washington, D.C.: National Academy of Engineering, Committee on Public Engineering Policy.

Cairns, J. 1975. "The Cancer Problem" *Scientific American* 233, no. 5: 64–78.

Calabresi, G. 1970. *The Cost of Accidents: A Legal and Economic Analysis.* New Haven, Connecticut: Yale University Press.

Caldwell, L. K., ed. 1968–1972. Science, Technology and Public Policy: A Selected and Annotated Bibliography, 3 vols. Bloomington, Indiana: Program in Public Policy for Science and Technology, Department of Government, Indiana University.

Carnow, B. W., and V. A. Carnow. 1973. "Air Pollution and the Concept of No Threshold." In *Advances in Environmental Science and Technology*, vol. 3, edited by J. N. Pitts and R. L. Metcalf. New York: John Wiley and Sons.

Cassell, E. J.; D. W. Wolter; J. D. Mountain; J. R. Diamond; I. M. Mountain; and J. R. McCarroll. 1968. "Reconsiderations of Mortality as a Useful Index of Environmental Factors to Health." *American Journal of Public Health* 58: 1653-1657.

Chiang, C. L. 1964. "A Stochastic Model of Competing Risks of Illness and Competing Risks of Death." In *Stochastic Models In Medicine and Biology*, edited by J. Gurland. Madison, Wisconsin: University of Wisconsin Press.

Cohen, J. J. 1971. "A Case for Benefit-Risk Analysis." In *Risk vs. Benefits: Solution or Dream?* pp. 51-52. Compendium of papers presented at symposium sponsored by Western Interstate Nuclear Board, Los Alamos Scientific Laboratory, November 11-12.

Dacy, D., and H. Kunreuther. 1969. *The Economics of Natural Disasters.* New York: The Free Press.

Darby, W. 1974. "The Philosophy of Acceptable Risk and the Practicality of Maximum Safety." In *Environment and Quality of Food*, edited by P. L. White and D. Robbis. Mt. Kiskoe, New York: Futura Publishing Company.

Dasgupta, A. K., and D. W. Pearce. 1972. *Cost-Benefit Analysis.* New York: Harper & Row.

deHeer, H. J. 1973. "Calculating How Much Safety is Enough." *Chemical Engineering* 80, no. 4: 121-128.

DeShmukh, S. S. 1974. "Risk Analysis." *Chemical Engineering* 81, no. 13: 141-144.

Diamond, P. 1972. "Economic Factors in Benefit-Risk Decision Making." In *Perspectives on Benefit-Risk Decision Making.* Washington, D. C.: National Academy of Engineering, Committee on Public Engineering Policy.

Doderlin, J. M. 1975. *The Rasmussen Report Re-Reviewed—A Critique of 'Preliminary Review of the AEC Reactor Safety Study' Prepared by the Union of Concerned Scientists-Sierra Club Joint Review Committee, November, 1974.* Kjeller, Norway: Institutt for Atomenergi, Kjeller Research Establishment.

Dorfman, R. F., ed. 1965. *Measuring Benefits of Government Investments.* Washington, D. C.: The Brookings Institution.

Drake A.; R. L. Keeney; and P. Morse, eds. 1972. *Analysis of Public Systems.* Cambridge, Massachusetts: MIT Press.

Drinan, R. S. J. 1975. "Nuclear Power and the Role of Congress." *Environmental Affairs* 4, no. 4: 595-628.

Dunster, J. 1973. "Costs and Benefits of Nuclear Power." *New Scientist* 60, no. 868: 192-194.

Dunster, H. J., and A. S. Mclean. 1970. "The Use of Risk Estimates in Setting and Using Basic Radiation Protection Standards." *Health Physics* 19, no. 1: 121.

Dworkin, J. 1974. "Global Trends in Natural Disasters, 1947-1973." Natural Hazard Research Working Paper No. 26. Boulder, Colorado: University of Colorado.

Epstein, S. S. 1978. *The Politics of Cancer.* San Francisco: Sierra Club Books.

Epstein, S. S. 1972. "Information Requirements for Determining the Benefits–Risk Spectrum." In *Perspectives on Benefit–Risk Decision Making.* Washington, D.C.: National Academy of Engineering, Committee on Public Engineering Policy.

Epstein, S. S., and R. D. Grundy, eds. 1974. *The Legislation of Product Safety.* Cambridge, Massachusetts: MIT Press.

Epstein, S. S., and M. L. Legator. 1971. *Mutagenicity of Pesticides.* Cambridge, Massachusetts: The MIT Press.

Erdmann, R. C. 1975. "Comments on the Risk/Benefit Methodology Workshop." In *Risk–Benefit Methodology and Application* (UCLA–ENG–7598), edited by D. Okrent. Los Angeles: School of Engineering and Applied Sciences, University of California.

Farmer, F. R. 1975. "Accident Probability Criteria." *Journal of The Institution of Nuclear Engineers* 16, no. 2: 44.

Farmer, F. R. 1967. "Reactor Safety and Siting: A Proposed Risk Criterion." *Nuclear Safety* 8, no. 6: 539–548.

Farmer, F. R. 1967. "Siting Criteria: A New Approach." In *Containment and Siting of Nuclear Power Plants.* Vienna: International Atomic Energy Agency.

Fay, J. A. 1973. "Unusual Fire Hazard of LNG Tanker Spills." *Combustion Science and Technology* 7, no. 2: 47–49.

Fay, J. A., and J. MacKenzie. 1972. "Cold Cargo." *Environment* 14, no. 9: 21.

Feingold, E. 1965. "The Great Cranberry Crisis." In *Government Regulation of Business: A Casebook*, edited by E. A. Bock. Englewood Cliffs, New Jersey: Prentice–Hall.

Foreman, H., ed. 1970. *Nuclear Power and the Public.* Minneapolis: University of Minnesota Press.

Fraumeni, J. F., ed. 1975. *Persons at High Risk of Cancer: An Approach to Cancer Etiology and Control.* New York: Academic Press.

Gibson, S. B. 1975. "The Use of Quantitative Risk Criteria in Hazard Analysis." In *Risk–Benefit Methodology and Application* (UCLA–ENG–7598), edited by D. Okrent. Los Angeles: School of Engineering and Applied Sciences, University of California.

Gilbert, J. P.; R. J. Light; and F. Mosteller. 1975. "Assessing Social Innovations: An Empirical Base for Policy." In *Benefit–Cost and Policy Analysis 1974*, edited by R. Zeckhauser and A. C. Harberger. Chicago, Illinois: Aldine Publishing Company.

Gillette, R. 1974. "Nuclear Safety: Calculating the Odds of Disaster." *Science* 185: 838–839.

Gillette, R. 1972. "Radiation Standards: The Last Word or at Least a Definitive One." *Science* 178: 966–967, 1012.

Green, A. E., and A. J. Bourne. 1972. *Reliability Technology.* London: John Wiley and Sons.

Green, H. P. 1975. "Legal and Political Dimensions of Risk–Benefit Methodology." In *Risk–Benefit Methodology and Application* (UCLA–ENG–7598), edited by D. Okrent. Los Angeles: School of Engineering and Applied Sciences, University of California.

Green, H. P. 1975. "The Risk–Benefit Calculus in Safety Determinations." *The George Washington Law Review* 43, no. 3: 791–808.

Green, H. P. 1973. "Nuclear Power, Risk, Liability and Indemnity." *Michigan Law Review* 71: 479–510.

Green, H. P. 1970. "The Risk–Benefit Calculus in Nuclear Power Licensing." In *Nuclear Power and the Public*, edited by H. Foreman. Minneapolis: University of Minnesota Press.

Green, H. P. 1968. "Safety Determinations in Nuclear Power Licensing: A Critical View." *Notre Dame Lawyer* 43, no. 5: 633.

Hardin, G. 1968. "The Tragedy of the Commons." *Science* 162: 1243–1248.

Haveman, R., and J. Margolis, eds. 1970. *Public Expenditure and Policy Analysis*. Chicago, Illinois: Markham.

Hetman, F. 1973. *Society and the Assessment of Technology*. Paris, France: Organization for Economic Cooperation and Development.

Heuser, F. W., and P. Homke. 1975. "Reliability Analysis and Its Application for Safety Assessment of Nuclear Plants." In *Risk–Benefit Methodology and Application* (UCLA–ENG–7598), edited by D. Okrent. Los Angeles: School of Engineering and Applied Sciences, University of California.

Hoel, D. 1972. "Representation of Mortality Data by Competing Risks." *Biometrics* 28: 475–488.

Hollaender, A., ed. 1971. *Chemical Mutagens.* New York: Plenum Press.

Jones–Lee, M. W. 1976. *The Value of Life: An Economic Analysis.* Chicago: University of Chicago Press.

Kallet, A., and F. J. Schlink. 1973. *100,000,000 Guinea Pigs.* New York: Vanguard.

Katz, D. L., and C. M. Sliepcevich. 1971. "LNG/Water Explosions: Cause and Effect." *Hydrocarbon Processing* 50, no. 11: 240.

Keeney, R. L., and H. Raiffa. 1976. *Decision Analysis with Multiple Conflicting Objectives.* New York: John Wiley and Sons.

Lane, J. M.; J. D. Miller; and J. N. Neff. 1971. "Smallpox and Smallpox Vaccination Policy." *Annual Review of Medicine* 22: 251–272.

Lave, L. B., and E. P. Seskin; with M. J. Chappie. 1977. *Air Pollution and Human Health.* Baltimore, Maryland: The Johns Hopkins University Press.

Lave, L. B., and L. Silverman. 1976. "Economic Costs of Energy Related Environmental Pollution." *Annual Review of Energy* 1: 601.

Lawless, E. 1976. *Technology and Social Shock.* New Brunswick, New Jersey: Rutgers University Press.

Lifton, R. J. 1967. *Death in Life—Survivors of Hiroshima.* New York: Vantage Books.

Lifton, R. J., and E. Olson. 1974. *Living and Dying.* New York: Praeger.

Loomis, T. A. 1968. *Essentials of Toxicology.* Philadelphia: Lea and Febiger.

Mantel, N., and W. R. Bryan. 1961. "'Safety' Testing of Carcinogenic Agents." *Journal of the National Cancer Institute* 27, no. 2: 455–470.

Mantel, N.; R. B. Neeti; C. C. Crown; J. L. Ciminera; and J. W. Tukey. 1961. "An Improved 'Mantel–Bryan' Procedure for 'Safety' Testing of Carcinogens." *Cancer Research* 35, no. 4: 865–872.

McDonald, G. C., and R. C. Schwing. 1973. "Instabilities of Regression Estimates Relating Air Pollution to Mortality." *Technometrics* 15: 463–481.

McKnight, A. D.; P. K. Marstrand; and J. C. Sinclair, eds. 1974. *Environmental Pollution Control: Technical, Economic and Legal Aspects.* London: Allen & Unwin.

Medford, D. 1973. *Environmental Harassment or Technology Assessment.* New York: Elsevier.

Merrill, R. A. 1977. "Risk–Benefit Decision Making by Food and Drug Administration." *George Washington Law Review* 45, no. 5: 994–1012.

Moll, K. S., et al. 1975. *Methods for Determining Acceptable Risks from Cadmium, Asbestos and Other Hazardous Wastes.* Menlo Park, California: Stanford Research Institute.

Muntzing, L. M. 1976. "Siting and Environment: Essentials in an Effective Nuclear Siting Policy." *Energy Policy* 4, no. 1: 3–11.

National Academy of Engineering, Committee on Public Engineering Policy. *Perspectives on Benefit–Risk Decision Making.* Washington, D. C.

National Academy of Sciences. 1976. *Pest Control: An Assessment of Present and Alternative Technologies.* Washington, D. C.

National Academy of Sciences. 1975. *Decision Making for Regulating Chemicals in the Environment.* Washington, D. C.

National Academy of Sciences, First Academy Forum. 1974. *How Safe is Safe? The Design of Policy on Drugs and Food Additives.* Washington, D. C.

National Academy of Sciences. 1970. *Evaluating the Safety of Food Chemicals.* Washington, D. C.

National Fire Protection Association. 1975. *Standard for the Production, Storage and Handling of Liquefied Natural Gas (LNG)* (NFPA No. 59A). Boston, Massachusetts.

National Highway Traffic Safety Administration. 1972. *Societal Costs of Motor Vehicle Accidents* (Preliminary Report). Washington, D. C.: U. S. Department of Transportation.

National Research Council. 1974. *Safety of Saccharin and Sodium Saccharin in the Human Diet.* Washington, D. C.

Nelkin, D. 1974. "The Role of Experts in a Nuclear Siting Controversy." *Bulletin of the Atomic Scientists* 30, no. 9: 29–36.

Nelson, W. "Hazard Plotting for Analysis of Life Data with Different Failure Modes." *Journal of Quality Technology* 2, no. 3: 126–149.

Okrent, D. 1977. *A General Evaluation Approach to Risk-Benefit for Large Technological Systems and Its Applications to Nuclear Power—Final Report* (UCLA-ENG-7777). Los Angeles: School of Engineering and Applied Sciences, University of California.

Okrent, D., and C. Whipple. 1977. *An Approach to Societal Risk Acceptance Criteria and Risk Management* (UCLA-ENG-7746). Los Angeles: School of Engineering and Applied Sciences, University of California.

Opinion Research Corporation. 1975. "Public Attitudes Toward Environmental Trade-Offs." *ORC Public Opinion Index* 33 (August): 1-8.

Otway, H. J. 1971. "The Quantification of Social Values." In *Risk vs. Benefit: Solution or Dream?* Compendium of papers presented at symposium sponsored by Western Interstate Nuclear Board, Los Alamos Scientific Laboratory, November 11-12.

Otway, H. J., and R. C. Erdmann. 1970. "Reactor Siting and Design from a Risk Viewpoint." *Nuclear Engineering Design* 13, no. 2: 365.

Otway, H. J., and P. D. Pahner. 1976. "Risk Assessment." *Futures* 8: 122-134.

Price, D. K. 1965. *The Scientific Estate.* Cambridge, Massachusetts: Harvard University Press.

Primack, J., and F. von Hippel. 1974. *Advice and Dissent: Scientists in the Political Arena.* New York: Basic Books.

Prusynski, M. S. 1977. "Risk Benefit Analysis and Technology Forcing Under the Toxic Substances Control Act." *Iowa Law Review* 62, no. 3: 942-959.

Rappaport, E. 1974. *Economic Analysis of Life-and-Death Decision-Making* (Appendix 2 in UCLA-ENG-7478). Los Angeles: School of Engineering and Applied Sciences, University of California.

Reynolds, D. J. 1956. "The Cost of Road Accidents." *Journal of the Royal Statistical Society* 119: 393-708.

Rice, D. P., and B. Cooper. 1967. "Economic Value of Human Life." *American Journal of Public Health* 57: 1954.

Rivard, J. B. 1971. "Risk Minimization by Optimum Allocation of Resources Available for Risk Reduction." *Nuclear Safety* 12: 305-309.

Rose, D. 1973. "An Investigation of Dependent Competing Risks." Ph.D. Dissertation, Department of Biostatistics, University of Washington, Seattle.

Rowe, W. D. 1977. *An Anatomy of Risk.* New York: Wiley-Interscience.

Sagan, L. A. 1972. "Human Costs of Nuclear Power." *Science* 177: 487-493.

Shapiro, J. 1972. *Radiation Protection.* Cambridge, Massachusetts: Harvard University Press.

Shneidman, E. S. 1974. *Deaths of Man.* Baltimore, Maryland: Penguin Books.

Siebert, C. D., and M. A. Zaidi. 1975. "Benefit/Cost Analysis in Health Care." *Biosciences Communications* 1, no. 4: 193-218.

Simmons, J. A.; R. C. Erdmann; and B. N. Naft. 1974. *The Risk of Catastrophic Spills of Toxic Chemicals* (UCLA-ENG-7425). Los Angeles: School of Engineering and Applied Sciences, University of California.

Solomon, K. A.; R. C. Erdmann; T. E. Hicks; and D. Okrent. 1974. *Airplane Crash Risk to Ground Population* (UCLA-ENG-7424). Los Angeles: School of Engineering and Applied Sciences, University of California.

Solomon, K. A.; R. C. Erdmann; G. S. Lellouche; and D. Okrent. 1975. "Additional Comments on Estimates of Hazards to a Nuclear Reactor from the Random Impact of Meteorites." *Nuclear Technology* 27: 528-530.

Solomon, K. A.; R. C. Erdman; and D. Okrent. 1975. "Estimate of Hazards to a Nuclear Reactor from Random Impact of Meteorites." *Nuclear Technology* 21, no. 1: 68.

Solomon, K. A.; M. Rubin; and D. Okrent. 1976. *On Risks from the Storage of Hazardous Chemicals* (UCLA-ENG-76125). Los Angeles: School of Engineering and Applied Sciences, University of California.

Starr, C.; M. A. Greenfield; and D. F. Hausknecht. 1972. "A Comparison of Public Health Risks: Nuclear vs. Oil-Fired Power Plants." *Nuclear News* 15, no. 10: 37.

Starr, C.; R. Rudman; and C. Whipple. 1976. "Philosophical Basis for Risk Analysis." *Annual Review of Energy* 1: 629.

Stokinger, H. E. 1972. "Concepts of Thresholds in Standard Setting." *Archives of Environmental Health* 25: 153-157.

Terrill, J. G. 1972. "Cost-Benefit Estimates for the Major Sources of Radiation Exposure." *American Journal of Public Health* 62, no. 7: 1008-1013.

Thaler, R., and S. Rosen. 1973. *The Value of Saving a Life: Evidence From the Labor Market.* Rochester, New York: Department of Economics, University of Rochester.

Tukey, J. W.; et al. 1973. *Chemicals and Health.* Report of the Panel on Chemicals and Health of the President's Science Advisory Committee. Washington, D.C.: U.S. Government Printing Office (Stock No. 3800-00159).

Turner, J. 1970. *The Chemical Feast: Report on the Food and Drug Administration.* New York: Grossman.

Tversky, A. 1975. "On the Elicitation of Preferences: Descriptive and Prescriptive Considerations." In *Proceedings of the Workshop on Decision Making with Multiple Conflicting Objectives.* Laxenburg, Austria: International Institute for Applied Systems Analysis.

Tversky, A., and D. Kahneman. 1973. "Availability: A Heuristic for Judging Frequency and Probability." *Cognitive Psychology* 5: 207-232.

Tversky, A., and D. Kahneman. 1971. "Belief in the Law of Small Numbers." *Psychological Bulletin* 76: 105-110.

U.S. Department of Health, Education and Welfare. 1976. *Cancer Rates and Risks.* DHEW Publication No. (NIH) 76-691. Washington, D.C.

U.S. Environmental Protection Agency, Office of Radiation Programs. 1976. *Reactor Safety Study (WASH-1400): A Review of the Final Report* (EPA-520/3-76/009). Washington, D.C.: Government Printing Office.

Van Horn, A. J., and R. Wilson. 1971. "The Pitfalls of Risk/Benefit Analysis: Critical Summaries of Selected Studies." Unpublished paper, Energy and Environmental Policy Center, Harvard University.

Van Horn, A. J., and R. Wilson. 1976. "The Potential Risks of Liquefied Natural Gas." Unpublished paper, Energy and Environmental Policy Center, Harvard University.

Wagoner, J. K.; V. E. Archer; F. E. Lundin Jr.; D. A. Holaday; and J. W. Lloyd. 1965. "Radiation as the Cause of Lung Cancer Among Uranium Miners." *New England Journal of Medicine* 273: 185.

Weatherwax, R. K. 1975. "Virtues and Limitations of Risk Analysis." *Bulletin of the Atomic Scientists* 31, no. 7: 29-32.

Weaver, P. H. 1975. "The Hazards of Trying to Make Consumer Products Safer." *Fortune* 42, no. 1 (July): 133-140.

Weinberg, A. M. 1972. "Science and Trans-Science." *Minerva* 10: 209-222.

Weisbrod, B. A. 1971. "Costs and Benefits of Medical Research: A Case Study of Poliomyelitys." *Journal of Political Economy* 79: 527-544.

Weisbrod, B. A. 1961. "The Valuation of Human Capital." *Journal of Political Economy* 69: 425-436.

White, G. F. 1972. "Human Response to Natural Hazard." In *Perspectives on Benefit-Risk Decision Making*. Washington, D.C.: National Academy of Engineering, Council on Public Engineering Policy.

White, G. F. 1966. "Formation and Role of Public Attitudes." In *Environmental Quality in a Growing Economy.*, edited by H. Jarret. Baltimore, Maryland: The Johns Hopkins University Press.

Wiggins, J. H., Jr. 1974. "Toward a Coherent Natural Hazards Policy." *Civil Engineering* 44, no. 4: 74-76.

Wilson, D. G. 1967. "A Cost-Benefit Approach to Transportation Developments." *Mechanical Engineering* 89, no. 7: 86.

Wilson, J. R. 1963. *Margin of Safety.* Garden City, New York: Doubleday and Company, Inc.

Wilson, R. 1975. "Examples in Risk-Benefit Analysis." *Chemical Technology* 6: 604-607.

Wingender, H. J. 1978. "Risk Analysis of Radioactive Waste Management Systems in Germany." *Nuclear Technology* 39, no. 1: 18-24.

Ziman, J. M. 1968. *Public Knowledge: An Essay Concerning the Social Dimensions of Science.* Cambridge, England: Cambridge University Press.

Zimmerman, B. K. 1978. "Risk-Benefit Analysis—Cop-Out of Government Regulation." *Trial* 14, no. 2: 43-47.

INDEX

ABOUT THE AUTHORS

Richard Wilson is a Professor of Physics at Harvard University. He helped to start the Energy and Environmental Policy Center in 1973 and served as its director from 1975 through 1978. For the last ten years he has been involved with environmental concerns, especially with various environmental risks about which he has written many articles.

Edmund Crouch is a Research Associate in the Department of Physics at Harvard University, working in the Energy and Environmental Policy Center. He became interested in risk assessment after a Ph.D. in theoretical physics from Cambridge University and three years as a Research Assistant at the Cambridge Energy Research Group. His current main interest is in the evaluation of risks of cancer from chemicals.